MOUNTAIN BIKING
THE RENO-CARSON CITY AREA

Guide 13

by R. W. Miskimins

Photographs by Bette E. and R. W. Miskimins

Maps and Book Design by Claire Hiester

FINE EDGE
Productions
BISHOP, CALIFORNIA

ACKNOWLEDGMENTS

Many people have contributed to this project, and I am grateful to them all. Let me begin by thanking my family. They have paid the highest price and given the most support and assistance for my passions, preoccupations and absences. My three adult children— Erin, Ryan and Kevin— are all cyclists and have shared time on the trails with me. Most directly helpful as regards this book has been Erin, the most serious rider of the three. My wife Bette has assisted throughout the process of putting this guidebook together; she has been on numerous rides and has provided the bulk of the photography for this project. And as my proofreader, she is always challenged by the task of transforming my rough manuscripts into "something readable". In addition to my family, there are numerous people who have in some way contributed encouragement, assistance or information to this book. It would be impossible to name them all since it includes all the people I have ridden with over the past few years. However, deserving of special mention here are Rich Staley and Scott Taylor, two local expert riders who have provided invaluable assistance to the research necessary to put this book together.

DISCLAIMER

Mountain biking is a potentially dangerous sport in which serious injury and death can and do occur. Trails have numerous natural and man-made hazards and conditions are constantly changing. Most of the routes in this book are not signed or patrolled, and this book may contain errors or omissions. It is not a substitute for proper instructions, experience and preparedness.

The author, editor, publisher, and others associated with this book are not responsible for errors or omissions and do not accept liability for any loss or damage incurred from using this book. You must accept full and complete responsibility for yourself while biking in the backcountry.

ABOUT THE AUTHOR

R. W. (Ray) Miskimins is a clinical psychologist with a consulting practice for adolescents and adults, as well as a bicycle shop owner in Reno. He and his family, all avid cyclists, operate Great Basin Bicycles, a full-service bicycle business geared to the entire family. Over the last three decades, Miskimins has published over 60 books and articles on various subjects ranging from residential treatment for emotionally disturbed youth to whitewater rafting. With off-road exploring on his bicycle occupying a tremendous amount of his time over the past few years, it only remained that he put his discoveries, over 30 wonderful trails, into a guidebook for all to enjoy.

Author at work.

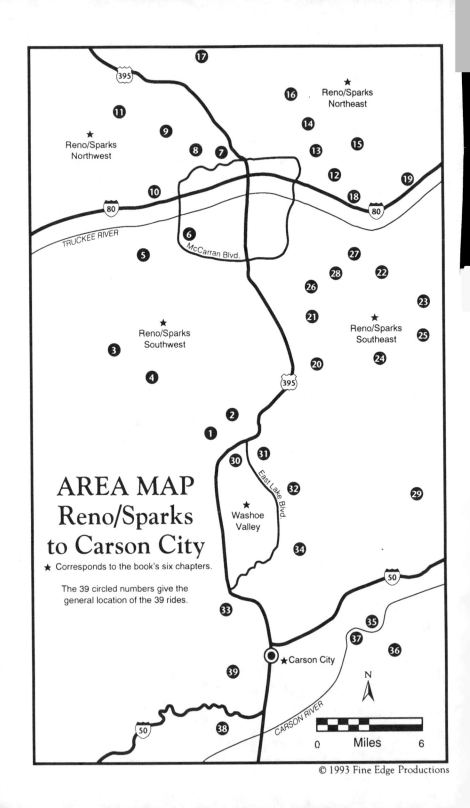

AREA MAP
Reno/Sparks
to Carson City

★ Corresponds to the book's six chapters.

The 39 circled numbers give the
general location of the 39 rides.

© 1993 Fine Edge Productions

TABLE OF CONTENTS

RIDE MAP LEGEND

Bike Route — — — —	● **START/FINISH**	⊙ *Gaging Station*	✈ *Airport*
Road ————————	▲ **MOUNTAIN PEAK**	▲ *Campground*	★ *Viewpoint*
Freeway ————————	⚐ *School*	○ *Water Tank*	)(*Bridge*
Power Lines — — — —	◎ *Radio Tower*	✕ *Gravel/Sand Pit*	─< *Tunnel*
River ————————	■ *Building/Parking*	⊡ *Petroglyphs/Site*	↳ *Golf*
Railroad ┼┼┼┼┼┼┼		△ *Rocky Knoll, Hill*	✗ *Mining*

INTRODUCTION

Due to the climate, the hills and the "wild west" outdoor attitude of Nevadans, mountain biking is extremely popular in the northern part of the state. Most of the population lives in the Truckee Meadows, or Washoe and Eagle valleys, each pretty much surrounded by mountain ranges. There is always the option of riding in one of the valleys or picking a nearby hill and trying to climb it. The popular mountain bike rides for the Reno-Carson City area, including the 39 offered in this guidebook, provide a lot of variety in terrain— from tall pine forests, to juniper and scrub pine covered highlands, to sagebrush covered hills, to barren dry lake beds. Generally, heading west from the valleys leads to the pine forests and heading east will take you to more arid country. The elevations available for the rides described in this guidebook range from 4400 to over 8000 feet. Included as features of interest are sites of several now extinct mining towns and cattle ranches, 3000 year-old Native American petroglyphs, lakes (both wet and dry), creeks, springs, a couple of rivers, and numerous fantastic views of both mountains and valleys. One thing for sure about the state of Nevada— there is a remarkable amount of unpopulated, open territory, making it a great place to ride a mountain bike!

Bridge over Brown's Creek.

1. COURTESY
A key to continued use of many of the roads/trails described in this book is courtesy to others with whom mountain bikers must share the trail. We are the newcomers; the hikers, joggers, hunters and equestrians have been there for decades. Please refer to Appendix A for the rules of the trail that have been offered by the International Mountain Bicycling Association (IMBA). Basically they ask that cyclists ride only on open trails, leave no trace, stay under control, always yield the trail, never spook animals (domestic or wild), and plan ahead. Regarding animals, many of the trails in this guidebook are regularly used by Northern Nevada's large population of recreational horse riders, and some of their horses are easily spooked. A startled horse can cause injuries to itself and its rider. When confronted by oncoming horses, stop and stand in full view off to the side of the trail to let them pass. If you come up behind horses, stop well behind them and don't pass until you

have alerted their riders and gotten permission to pass (and then pass very slowly). Always be alert to these various issues of courtesy and we can stop further closure of trails to mountain bikes.

2. RESPECT THE ENVIRONMENT

All recreationists who use the outdoors, from 4-wheel drive enthusiasts to backpackers, should work to minimize human and/or vehicle impact on the environment. Cyclists on mountain bikes should stay on established roads and trails, and not ride in very wet and muddy conditions. Leave plants and animals alone. Leave historic and cultural sites untouched. And remember, mountain bikes are not allowed in designated Wilderness Areas.

3. PREPARATION

Take a little extra time before each ride to make sure you and your bike are ready. Many riders develop a check list to be certain that they have proper clothing, water, essential tools, and depending upon the particular ride, other necessities (map, compass, first aid supplies, energy food, spare bike parts, fanny pack, and so on). Regular maintenance and a pre-ride checkup for your bike can save a lot of grief from breakdowns 10 or 15 miles from civilization. Appendix B describes the fundamental checkups all riders should frequently give their bicycles.

4. DESERT CONDITIONS

Some parts of several of the rides described in this book involve open desert, where shade and water are virtually non-existent. In the summer be alert to what heat and sun can do to you, in the form of sunburn, heat exhaustion, UV eye irritation, and so on. For long rides, the standard two water bottles will not provide enough water for most people and severe dehydration can be deadly. Be aware that any desert water you find from springs, creeks or lakes is a potential source of giardiasis if you don't boil, filter or otherwise treat it. Wind is also a potential irritant for the cyclist, especially as it reaches high speed in open desert areas— it can add to skin irritation and both exhaust and dehydrate you quickly.

5. MOUNTAIN CONDITIONS

Some of Northern Nevada's rides go up into the mountains, to altitudes over 8000 feet. As described for desert conditions, the sun can present serious problems for the cyclist. And in the mountains, you add the possibility of more extreme temperature variations— you can go from extreme heat to extreme cold (or the reverse) in a brief period of time. Always be alert to existing weather patterns and to the necessity for having layers of clothing to put on or take off with significant changes in the temperature. And you should know how to recognize and deal with hypothermia, the result of poor preparation for low temperatures. Check with the local Red Cross, Sierra Club or outdoor recreation textbooks for detailed information on surviving both desert and mountain conditions.

6. SAFETY

The two prime keys to safe cycling on the mountain bike trails described in this guidebook are wearing a helmet and riding under control. Regarding the first, a large percentage of the serious injuries associated with cycling involve impact to the head. Fully approved (ANSI and Snell) helmets are extremely cheap when compared to an hour of a neurosurgeon's time— buy a helmet and wear it! Regarding the second point, control your mountain bike at all times. Here, the major problem is excessive speed. If you ride faster than the trail surface, your skills or your equipment can handle, the chance of a crash is greatly increased. Work on basic technical skills (see Appendix C), and don't go faster than your ability level.

7. CYCLIST FIRST AID

Carry basic first aid supplies, especially for long rides into uninhabited areas. At the very least, be prepared for wind/sun exposure and for cuts and scrapes ("road rash"). There are first aid kits designed specifically for cyclists, such as the "After the Fall" kit distributed by Atwater-Carey. Always be alert to the possibility of encountering rattlesnakes, especially on the desert rides when you are near a water source. Give them a wide berth, make some noise and they will usually retreat rapidly. If you are bitten, stay calm and get to the nearest hospital for treatment. For toxic insect bites or stings (spiders, scorpions, etc.), you should also immediately seek medical treatment. Finally, as noted earlier, be alert to the symptoms created by a human body that is having difficulty dealing with heat or cold, and know what you need to do about it.

8. BICYCLE FIRST AID

The most common off-road repair is a flat tire. Carry a spare tube, a patch kit, tire levers (the tools to remove tires), and a pump. Another possible problem is loosening of various parts (handlebar, stem, brake levers, saddle, water bottle cages, etc.)— for most bikes, carry allen wrenches, sizes 4, 5 and 6mm, to deal with these concerns. Other tools frequently carried by off-road cyclists includes socket wrenches (8, 9 and 10mm), crescent wrench, spoke wrench and a chain-breaker tool.

9. MAPS AND NAVIGATION

If you enjoy exploring far from human population, you should carry and know how to read a topo map and use a compass. The maps in this book are aids to route finding only and are not to be used for navigation. We recommend that you purchase and carry the USGS (United States Geological Survey) Topo map(s) listed in the heading for each ride. Warning: Not all the roads on the USGS maps are on the guidebook maps, and not all the roads/trails found on the maps in this guidebook are on the USGS maps! On some rides it is easy to get lost. Before you leave, tell someone where you're going and when you expect to return. En route, keep track of your position on a map and be aware of compass bearings at all times. Look back frequently in the direction from which you came, especially for those rides that follow an out and back route (a turn may look considerably different when approached from the opposite direction).

10. USING THIS GUIDEBOOK

There are 39 rides presented in this book. They represent most of the well-known, popular mountain bike trails in Northern Nevada. For each ride, a

"Difficulty" rating is given: Beginner, Intermediate, Advanced or Expert. These ratings are to give a general indication of such factors as elevation gain, roughness of the road/trail surface, distance, dangerous descents, and so on, with a single word descriptor. If a ride gets too tough for you, turn around and go back, walk parts of it, go slower, or whatever is necessary to assure your comfort and safety. Also, be aware that there are numerous factors (such as weather, recent road/trail repair, flooding, and so on) that can markedly change the Difficulty rating— judging how hard a ride is and deciding whether you can handle it ultimately must be your responsibility.

After Difficulty, each ride is prefaced by a "Distance" figure. This number tells the length of the ride (out and back or loop) without any sidetrips or exploration, and without connecting it to other nearby rides described in this guidebook. Distance effectively is the minimum mileage for any particular ride. Following Distance are "Starting Elevation" and "Highest Elevation"— if the Starting Elevation is not the lowest altitude for the ride, it will be noted in the text. The majority of the rides in the Reno-Carson City area involve climbing up into the hills adjacent to the two cities and elevations are given to indicate the intensity of the uphill for each. The last form of information prefacing the rides in this guidebook is "Map". Given here is the USGS map (or maps) which cover each ride. This information is presented in order that cyclists may purchase them, especially if they want to explore beyond the basic route given herein.

Stop for roadside repairs.

CHAPTER 1 RENO/SPARKS SOUTHWEST

Ride #1 Joy Lake; #2 Galena Loop; #3 Hunter Lake Climb; #4 Thomas Creek Climb, #5 West Hills Climb; #6 Steamboat Ditch Trail.

Riding west from Reno takes you into the pine-covered slopes of the Carson Range. (The Sierra Nevada Range, itself, lies directly west of the Carson Range.) With the exception of Steamboat Ditch Trail that runs along the edge of the valley, the routes in this chapter include areas forested by tall ponderosa pines and are particularly desirable during summer months when cool temperatures and shade are at a premium.

Ride #1
JOY LAKE

Difficulty: Intermediate
Distance: 9 1/2 miles
Starting Elevation: 5450 feet
Highest Elevation: 5850 feet
Map: USGS Washoe City 7.5

Tall pines at Joy Lake.

Trailhead
From Reno, head south on U.S. 395 for ten miles. At the Mt. Rose junction turn right (west, toward Lake Tahoe) and proceed four miles. Turn left onto Callahan Ranch Road and go about 1 1/2 miles to the State Historical Marker for Galena. There is space to park a few cars near the Galena sign.

Difficulty
If you complete the entire loop from the Galena marker to Cattlemen's (restaurant) on U.S. 395 at the north end of Washoe Valley and back, with a side trip to Joy Lake, the 9 1/2 mile ride is best suited to intermediates and above. A shortened run from Galena to Joy Lake and back not only cuts off 4 miles

but eliminates the long climb out of Washoe Valley (the elevation at U.S. 395 is 5075, as compared to 5850 at Joy Lake). The ride to Joy Lake and back, without the descent to Cattlemen's, has only modest and gradual changes in elevation, and is suitable for most all riders.

Description
This ride offers access to one of the beautiful pine forests which border the Truckee Meadows. It is particularly desirable for summer days, when you would like a break from the hot, open

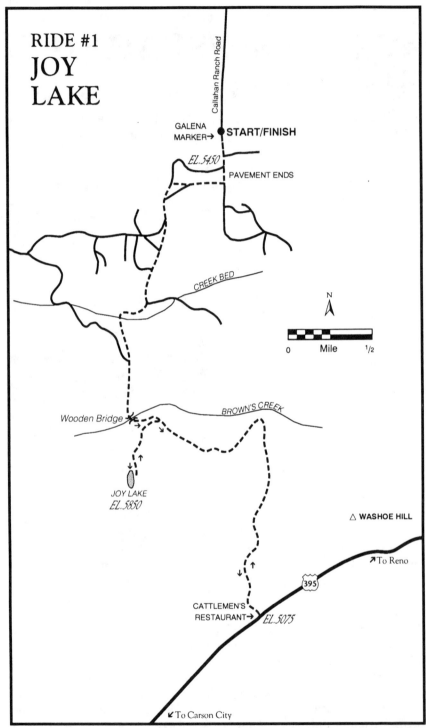

RIDE #1
JOY
LAKE

Callahan Ranch Road

GALENA
MARKER→ ●START/FINISH

EL.5450

PAVEMENT ENDS

CREEK BED

N

0   Mile   1/2

BROWN'S CREEK

Wooden Bridge

JOY LAKE
EL.5850

△ WASHOE HILL

↗To Reno

395

CATTLEMEN'S
RESTAURANT→ EL.5075

↙To Carson City

© 1993 Fine Edge Productions

desert. As you leave the Galena marker (headed south), in less than a quarter mile you will be on dirt roads and in the woods. Turn right at the first opportunity after the pavement ends and follow the main road (west) to a sloppy "T" where you have to swing left (south). At about three-quarters of a mile bear left at the "Y" (the road to the right goes to private homes). Continue south, pretty much straight ahead and staying on the main road. At just under a mile and one-half you will make a large U-turn (to the left) with a creek bed in the middle of the turn. Depending upon the time of year, this crossing varies from a dry wash to a foot-deep, fast flowing creek.

Continue south and you will cross a wooden bridge over Brown's Creek at two miles from Galena (and then the road swings east). At 2 1/4 miles you will encounter a side road, headed uphill to the right— this is the route to Joy Lake. It's about one-half mile to the lake. A little over one-quarter mile up this road is the entrance to a private camp and a sign for the "Whittell Audubon Center". When you reach the posted, fenced camp use the trail along the left fenceline to get to the water (or close). Do not disturb the habitat! The Joy Lake area is a great place for a rest stop. Look for some panoramic views of Washoe Valley and beyond.

To continue your ride, turn around and proceed back down to the main road, then head east and begin the two mile descent out of the trees and down to Cattlemen's. If you want to complete the 5 1/4 mile ride from Galena to Cattlemen's (mileage includes the one mile side trip to Joy Lake), but not ride this route in reverse (the full out and back, as noted earlier, is 9 1/2 miles), you need to have transportation awaiting you or you will have a 13 mile ride up U.S. 395, Mount Rose Highway and Callahan Ranch Road to get back to Galena.

Ride #2
GALENA LOOP

Difficulty: Beginner
Distance: 4 miles
Starting Elevation: 5450 feet
Highest Elevation: 5500 feet
Map: USGS Washoe City 7.5

Trailhead

From downtown Reno, go south on U.S. 395 for ten miles. At the Mt. Rose junction turn right (west on Highway 451, toward Lake Tahoe) and proceed up the Mt. Rose highway for four miles. Turn left onto Callahan Ranch Road and go about 1 1/2 miles to the State Historical Marker for Galena. There is space to park a few cars near the Galena sign.

Difficulty

This is a relatively short, non-technical ride, suitable for all levels of cyclists. Beginners will find it a pleasant one-hour ride with minimal climbing (the elevation change is only 210 feet for the entire loop). More advanced riders can do it in half that time and can increase the difficulty and workout by riding the four-mile loop several times. In addition, the ride can be expanded

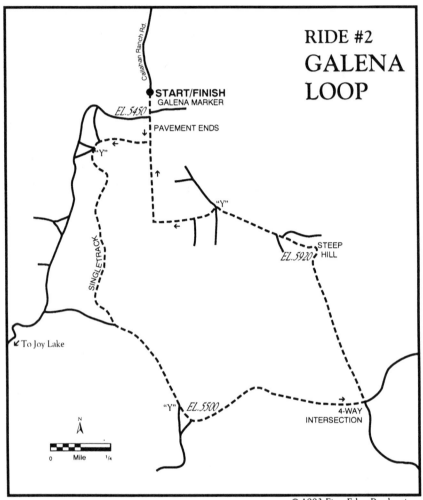

RIDE #2
GALENA LOOP

Callahan Ranch Rd

START/FINISH
GALENA MARKER

EL. 5450

PAVEMENT ENDS

"Y"

"Y"

SINGLETRACK

STEEP HILL
EL. 5920

To Joy Lake

"Y" EL. 5500

4-WAY INTERSECTION

N

0   Mile   1/4

by exploring some of the secondary roads and trails that intersect the loop.

Description

Galena was a settlement, established in the spring of 1860, that came into existence to produce timbers for the Comstock mining operation in Virginia City. All that remains today is a trace of the town's graveyard. Beginning at the Galena marker, ride south on Callahan Ranch Road. After the pavement ends, turn right (just under one-quarter mile from the start). At just under one—half a mile, just before the "Y", turn sharp left onto a single track. Follow the single track, ignoring intersecting trails, until it merges with a jeep road (at just under 1 1/4 miles). Continue ahead (south) on the road (a right turn here would take you west to intersect with the road to Joy Lake and

Cattlemen's Restaurant on U.S. 395). At one and two-thirds miles you will encounter a "Y"— bear left. At just over two miles is a 4-way intersection. Turn left and head north. One-half mile later take the road to the right. If you miss this turn you will very soon thereafter have to ride down a short but very steep hill— the road to the right loops around and ends up at the base of the hill. Continue ahead from the steep hill, almost immediately turning left at the powerlines (3 miles from the start). Follow the main road, bearing left at the "Y". Continue west on the main road and take the sharp right turn at 3 1/2 miles. From this turn go north for one-half mile, which will return you to the Galena historical marker (for a total of 4 miles).

Ride #3
HUNTER LAKE CLIMB

Difficulty: Expert
Distance: 14 1/2 miles
Starting Elevation: 5240 feet
Highest Elevation: 8260 feet
Map: USGS Mt. Rose NE/Mt. Rose NW 7.5

Trailhead
Take West McCarran to Cashill/ Caughlin Parkway and go west on Caughlin. Go past the shopping center and past "Village Green Pkwy". Turn left on "Village Green Pk" (one block past the "Pkwy") and go past the Caughlin Ranch Elementary School. One-fourth mile past the school, turn right onto a dirt road leading up to a power substation. Park along the dirt

road, just off the pavement.

Difficulty
This ride, climbing high up into the Carson Range, is very popular with the area's most accomplished mountain bikers. It is variously described, in terms ranging from exciting to horrible, depending upon the rider's fitness, technical riding skills, and attitudes regarding physical discomfort. Due to its length (14 1/2 miles), the elevation gain to get from the edge of the valley up to the lake (3000 feet), and the extreme rockiness of parts of the road, the Hunter Lake Climb is suited to expert riders.

Description
It is important to carefully follow the instructions for the early part of this ride— it begins in a maze of jeep trails. Generally, you need to maintain a southwesterly direction for most of the ride (and to make sure you don't get lost, always be aware of your general compass bearings). Begin the Hunter Lake Climb by taking the dirt road up to the Mt. Rose Substation. As you reach the substation swing right (southwest)— after you go right you can see the road you want ahead of you, leading up to the trees. At one-half mile you will reach a sharp switchback to the left. About 200 yards later you will come up onto a large dirt flat, a multiroad intersection. Go 90 degrees left (uphill, directly to the west). At just under one mile, go left at the "T" (continue uphill). At just over one mile, go left at the fork— there are two parallel roads, very close together, headed west (take either). A few hundred feet later, when the two roads come back to-

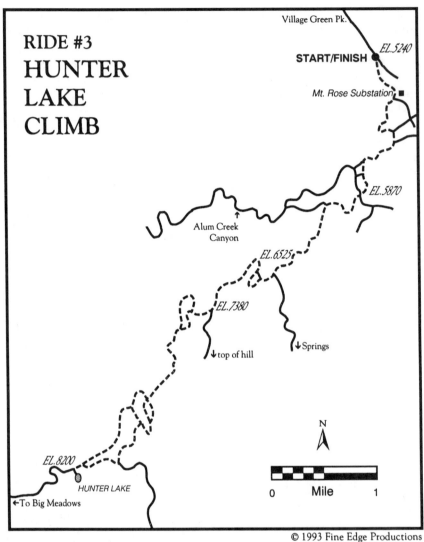

RIDE #3
HUNTER LAKE CLIMB

Village Green Pk.

START/FINISH

EL.5240

Mt. Rose Substation

EL.5870

Alum Creek Canyon

EL.6525

EL.7380

↓top of hill

↓Springs

EL.8200

HUNTER LAKE

←To Big Meadows

N

0   Mile   1

© 1993 Fine Edge Productions

gether, don't turn right up the steep hill (keep going straight ahead). Through this section and ahead at the next flat are great views of the Truckee Meadows.

At just under 1 1/2 miles you will ride up onto another flat with multiple roads. If you want a shorter ride than the one to Hunter Lake, you can turn sharp right at this intersection and go north (then west) around the hill in front of you and explore Alum Creek Canyon (it will be on your right after you swing around the hill and there is a turn to your left after about a mile which loops back to the Hunter Lake road). If you take the Alum Creek road until it ends, you can see down into Hunter Creek Canyon. Be warned that the last mile or so involves some steep climbing and is not suitable to beginners.

For those riders continuing up to Hunter Lake, don't take the sharp right to Alum Creek Canyon— instead, bear right to take you up and over the corner of the hill in front of you. This climb is extremely rocky and steep. Partway up the hill you can take either road (both are bad). At just under 2 3/4 miles you must bear right at the fork (left goes due south to some springs). At three miles you will pass a green wrecked car on your left. Shortly thereafter, the road forks—take either. You are now headed north, but shortly you will swing left (and soon be riding in a southwesterly direction again). Continue on the main road, bearing left if you have choices; your route will take you through a large clearing. At just under 4 1/2 miles (in the clearing) stay right at the fork (left leads to a dead end at the top of the hill). At 4 1/2 miles, stay left (look up on the ridge and you will see the road that you soon will be on). At just under 4 3/4 miles, the two roads you encountered at 4 1/2 miles converge and you begin over one-half mile of extremely rocky riding. Continue ahead on the main road, bearing right at choice points.

At just under 5 1/2 miles (you will again be in a large opening), look straight ahead and you can see the last climb before the downhill to Hunter Lake (the main road first goes left/south, then switchbacks to the right/north). There are multiple roads in this last section, all either circling back to the main road or leading to the lake, but the turns below give the best route.

A few hundred yards past 5 1/2 miles go left at the fork, then almost immediately go right at the next fork— stay on the main road (you are now headed south).

At 6 1/4 miles stay right on the main road (left takes you over the ridge onto a very rocky road). Along here look to the right for a fantastic view. At 6 1/3 miles you pass a very large boulder (about the size of a UPS van) on your immediate left and shortly thereafter the road goes west and south downhill, then flattens out headed west to Hunter Lake.

At 7 1/4 miles go left (about 100 feet) through the trees into an open valley containing Hunter Lake. This little lake and the creek below it were named after John M. Hunter, a man who owned a toll bridge across the Truckee River in the late 1860's— it was at the site of his bridge that Virginia City stages met the Central Pacific Railroad. After a break here at this football field size lake, for a 14 1/2 mile out and back ride, turn around and retrace your route back

Rocky road to Hunter Lake.

to the power substation. For the hardy, an alternate route back involves continuing on the road that brought you to Hunter Lake. You have to go west a little over two miles to an area called Big Meadows, and shortly thereafter head north. You will ride past a radio facility (on your left) and ultimately end up directly across I-80 from Boomtown— from here you have to ride along the freeway to McCarran, then take McCarran south to get back to where you started.

Ride #4
THOMAS
CREEK CLIMB

Difficulty: Intermediate
Distance: 7 miles
Starting Elevation: 5700 feet
Highest Elevation: 6780 feet
Map: USGS Mt. Rose NE/Mt. Rose NW 7.5

Trailhead
Heading south from Reno on U.S. 395, drive 10 miles to the Mt. Rose Junction and turn right onto Highway 431. Head west on this road for 5 1/2 miles, then turn right onto North Timberline (at the base of the steep hill, about one-half mile past the fire station). Park at the turn, in the vicinity of the large signs saying "Timberline".

Difficulty
This ride is for intermediates and above. It does not demand high-level technical skills but be aware that there is the possibility of problems from downhilling too fast. For 3 1/2 miles the climb is relentless and sometimes fairly steep— the total elevation gain is 1000 feet.

Description
This ride is seven miles long, 3 1/2 miles out and back by the same route. It starts on the edge of the desert and goes well up into the mountains. The last couple of miles provide lots of scenery with a year-round creek, towering pines, quaking aspen, numerous wildflowers and shrubs, and mini-meadows. Starting at the intersection of Mt. Rose Highway and North Timberline, go north into the housing development, along the base of the steep hill on your left. Continue north when the pavement ends. At just over one-half mile ride over the bridge crossing Whites Creek and continue north.

At just over one mile you will cross Thomas Creek and encounter three roads. The one to the right only goes for about one-fourth mile (along the creek). The one straight ahead follows the foothills north and can take you to Reno— this route is very rocky through long stretches and riding it can be very unpleasant (it has been dubbed "the Road from Hell"). Bear left to head uphill alongside Thomas Creek. Almost immediately you will be in the trees. If you need stopping places, for the next couple of miles there are numerous primitive campgrounds on your left beside the creek.

At just over 1 1/2 miles the road splits around two pine trees. Continue on up the hill. At two miles the road splits around a single pine tree. For the next three-quarters of a mile there are flat, sometimes grassy areas on the left, then

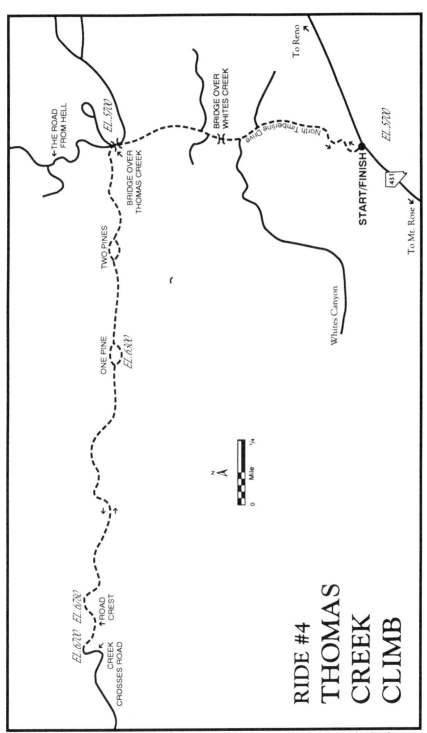

RIDE #4
THOMAS
CREEK
CLIMB

© 1993 Fine Edge Productions

the road steepens as you climb up the right side of a deep canyon.

Just short of 3 1/2 miles, at a crest in the road, is a four way intersection. Two of the roads are gated and lead into private property. Go ahead left and down to Thomas Creek. This is the turnaround and an extremely scenic spot for a rest break.

Depending upon the creek's water level and your endurance, it is possible to continue ahead through the creek and resume your westward climb for another mile or so. The road goes much farther, all the way up to the springs high in the Carson Range which feed the creek and beyond (gaining almost another 3000 feet in elevation), but bicycles are not allowed in the Mt. Rose Wilderness area.

Ride #5
WEST HILLS CLIMB

Difficulty: Intermediate
Distance: 7 1/2 miles
Starting Elevation: 4900 feet
Highest Elevation: 5600 feet
Map: USGS Mt. Rose NW 7.5

Trailhead
From South Virginia (about two miles south of downtown), take Plumb Lane west. Go past McCarran, past Caughlin Club and turn right on Longknife. Follow the winding subdivision street to the intersection of Longknife and Plateau (about one-half mile). Turn right

on Plateau, follow it for about one-half mile, then turn left onto Woodchuck and park your vehicle.

Difficulty
Most of the first half of this 7 1/2 mile ride (a little over three and one-half miles each direction, out and back) is a steady climb. From the point at which you are near the Steamboat Ditch (elevation 4900 feet) you will climb to about 5600 feet. Because this ride is short and has only a few fairly brief "technical" sections, it is suitable for intermediate level riders. When having difficulty (especially on rocky downhills) you can always get off your bike and walk.

Description
This ride begins on a wide dirt road, then courses along Hunter Creek to a gaging station, then follows a jeep trail up to the trees. Beginning on Woodchuck, ride up the unpaved road which angles off to the right. At one-half mile the road narrows and swings right through a short (about 50 feet in length) rocky section. Immediately after the rocky part turn right and go

Sagebrush-lined jeep trail.

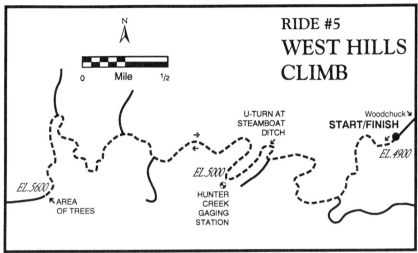

downhill and through another rocky section. When you encounter Steamboat Ditch (at three-fourths of a mile, next to chain-link fenced water routing area), make a U-turn left and head back up the canyon. Hunter Creek will now be on your left. At 1 1/4 miles the road crosses a wash. You will soon reach the gaging station where there is a hiking trail straight ahead into the Mt. Rose Wilderness (bicycles are prohibited). At the gaging station, make the hairpin turn to the right and head up the hill. Stay on the main road for the next couple of miles (avoid side roads headed sharply uphill or downhill). At just over three miles you will encounter a fork. Essentially, the road you have been following is on the right and goes straight ahead (and downhill), the other fork swings sharply left and heads uphill. Go left and after one-half mile (a total of 3 3/4 miles) you will cross under power lines. This ride ends a few hundred yards later— you have reached the trees! After a break to enjoy the wonderful view from this hillside, you

Always wear a helmet!

turn around and retrace your route back to Woodchuck. For the hardy there are some options here to lengthen the ride. If you take the road under the power lines downhill, it is possible to connect with various other roads (or the Steamboat Ditch). You also have the option of not turning around when you reach the trees, and continuing on to the west for several miles.

Ride #6
STEAMBOAT DITCH TRAIL

Difficulty: Beginner
Distance: 43 miles
Elevation Range: 4600 to 5000 feet
Map: USGS Mt. Rose NW/Verdi/Mt.
    Rose NE/Steamboat 7.5

Trailhead

The Steamboat Ditch Trail has been embroiled in considerable controversy over the past few years. The Steamboat Ditch is a 43 mile long canal, finished in 1878, carrying water for irrigation. The water is drawn from the Truckee River, from just above Verdi (near the mouth of the Truckee River Canyon). The ditch ends just south of the Steamboat Hot Springs (off of U.S. 395, about a mile south of the Mt. Rose Highway/Geiger Grade junction). It is these natural hot springs that gave the ditch the name Steamboat (regarding the hot springs, Mark Twain in 1863 wrote that "one can hear a constant rumbling and surging, somewhat resembling the noises peculiar to a steamboat in motion— hence the name").

Any remaining water from Steamboat Ditch flows into Steamboat Creek, a waterway which ultimately empties into Little Washoe Lake at the north end of Washoe Valley. Alongside most of the canal is the "trail", a primitive road which provides access for the Steamboat Ditch and Irrigation Company for maintenance purposes— their right to that access is protected by easement.

For many decades, even though the Steamboat Ditch Trail courses primarily across private land and the easements are for the Ditch Company, hikers and equestrians (and recently mountain bikers) have used the roadway as if it were public. Despite the fact the ditch trail goes through populated areas and the level of use there has been remarkably high, until recently there were virtually no problems involving access. If you choose to ride portions of the Steamboat Ditch Trail today, you will find some parts of it generally open (e.g., through the Caughlin Ranch housing development or on National Forest Service property), and some parts of it generally closed (e.g., through Lakeridge Golf Course or north off of South McCarran). Recently, one Reno couple granted their ditch easement to the Nevada Trust for Public Lands, to ultimately be given to the City of Reno, in order to preserve Steamboat Ditch Trail. It appears others will soon follow suit. If you wish to ride the ditch trail, be cognizant of the fact you may be limited in access or distance by individual property owners or the Steamboat Ditch and Irrigation Company. Please respect all gates, fences and signs placed to limit entry.

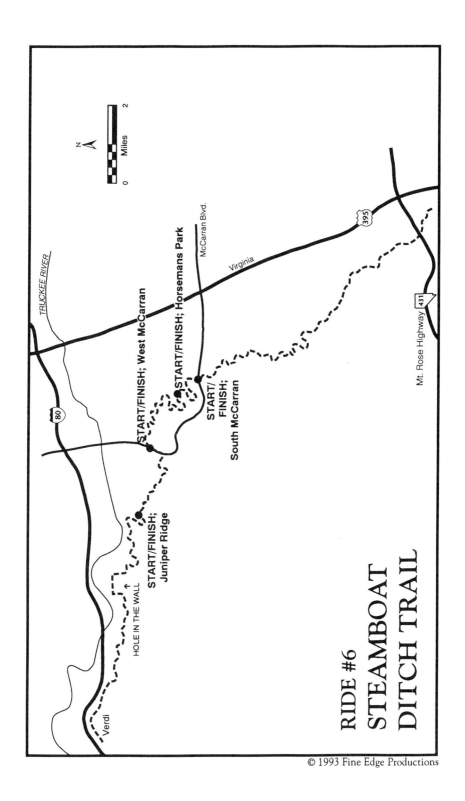

RIDE #6
STEAMBOAT
DITCH TRAIL

TRUCKEE RIVER

START/FINISH; West McCarran

START/FINISH; Horsemans Park

START/
FINISH;
South McCarran

START/FINISH;
Juniper Ridge

HOLE IN THE WALL

Verdi

McCarran Blvd.

Virginia

Mt. Rose Highway

80

395

431

N

0   Miles   2

Listed below are the four most popular "trailheads," starting points for riding the Steamboat Ditch Trail— each has two access points, depending upon whether you head upstream or downstream.

(1) South McCarran: Take McCarran about two miles west of South Virginia Street and watch for where the ditch goes under the highway.

(2) Horsemans Park: Go west on Moana from South Virginia Street, then left (south) on Skyline for a little over 1/2 mile.

(3) West McCarran: From where McCarran crosses the Truckee River, go south (up the hill) about 1 1/2 miles and watch for where the ditch goes under the highway.

(4) Juniper Ridge Subdivision: From south Virginia Street, take Plumb west. Go past McCarran, past the Caughlin Club and turn right on Longknife. Follow the winding subdivision streets to the intersection of Longknife and Plateau (about 1/2 mile). Turn right on Plateau and follow it for about a mile (you can see the ditch on your left as you drive the last 1/2 mile).

Difficulty

Virtually all the Steamboat Ditch Trail is on flat, slightly bumpy terrain, well suited to riders of all levels. It provides a close-to-town, aerobic mountain bike experience without demanding technical riding skills or superior physical conditioning.

Description

Although the surface of this trail varies very little, the surrounding terrain varies remarkably depending upon what part of the 43-mile length you are on.

Much of the central portion is alongside closely packed together homes— the level of use here is very high because of the trail's proximity to tens of thousands of people. South of the central portion is more open, but still near numerous homes.

The most popular (and lately, most controversial) portion of the trail for cyclists has been the section west of the central portion. The part west of Caughlin Ranch, once you are past Hunter Creek and the Juniper Ridge subdivision, has a very rural feeling— there are no homes in sight and you have the possibility of seeing deer, mustangs, coyotes, rattlesnakes, and other wild creatures. About a mile and one-half west of Hunter Creek you will encounter "Mike's Point" (identified by a sign next to a small gravesite), a scenic overlook of the Truckee River. It is three miles west of here that most cyclists turn around— you will encounter "Hole in the Wall" (the waterway goes into a mountain, tunneling through a hill). If you don't want to U-turn, it is possible to walk/ride up and over the steep hill in front of you or to bear right (between the fence posts) and follow the road along the side of the hill and then downhill to a "T". At this intersection, turn left and proceed down to the river— a scenic spot for a snack stop. This side trip from the Steamboat Ditch Trail, like most of those sidetrips that are available along the ditch, is not suited to beginner riders. As soon as you leave the ditch trail, the roads are more rocky and are usually quite steep uphill or downhill.

CHAPTER 2 RENO/SPARKS NORTHWEST

Ride # 7 Rancho San Rafael Park Canyon; #8 Keystone Canyon Loop; #9 Poeville Canyon Climb; #10 Ring Around the Golf Course; #11 Peavine Peak Climb.

The area north of downtown Reno— where a single peak, Peavine Mountain, dominates the skyline— offers a number of possibilities for exploration by mountain bike. This chapter describes the five most popular rides in the sector. A maze of primitive trails, created over the years by 4-wheel drive trucks and other motorized off-road vehicles, give cyclists of all abilities a wide variety of choices. Although most cyclists confine their riding to the lower portions of the mountain on the south side, the most popular route is the Peavine Peak Climb. You can ride to the summit from several different starting points, and the view at the top rewards you for all your climbing efforts.

Ride #7 RANCHO SAN RAFAEL PARK CANYON

Difficulty: Beginner
Distance: 3 1/4 miles
Starting Elevation: 4750 feet
Highest Elevation: 5000 feet
Map: USGS Reno 7.5

Trailhead

This ride, located in the southeastern foothills of Peavine Peak, has been given several names over the past few years. "Park Canyon" (or Rancho San Rafael Park Canyon) is probably the best because it identifies the starting point. The other commonly used name is "Lower Canyon"— those calling it by that name often call Keystone Canyon "Upper Canyon". The trailhead for the Park Canyon ride is on the north side of McCarran, at the western boundary of Rancho San Rafael Park (wide parking area next to a gate). From downtown Reno, go north on Virginia to North McCarran— turn left onto McCarran and drive west to the edge of the park. It is also possible to reach Park Canyon out of the park (ride past the large green statue, then turn right to go down into the canyon; join the described route just past the large wooden flume).

Difficulty

If you cycle up to the top of the canyon and back, this ride is suited to riders of all skill levels (with a little caution in rocky areas). The total distance is just over 3 miles and the total elevation gain is only 250 feet. It is possible to extend both the length and difficulty of the ride by climbing to the west once you reach the top of the canyon, and connect to other rides such as Keystone Canyon Loop— when the Park Canyon ride is extended, much higher

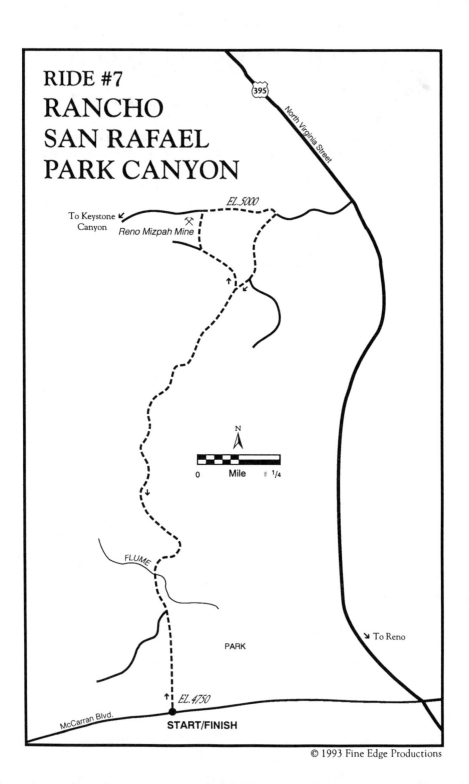

RIDE #7
RANCHO
SAN RAFAEL
PARK CANYON

EL.5000

To Keystone Canyon

Reno Mizpah Mine

395

North Virginia Street

N

0   Mile   1/4

FLUME

PARK

To Reno

EL.4750

McCarran Blvd.

START/FINISH

level technical skills and endurance are required and thus it is for intermediates or better.

Description

From the parking area on McCarran go through the gate and take the jeep road to the north. At one-third mile you will pass an interesting old wooden flume on your right. Immediately ahead is a large dirt flat— go straight, under the powerlines, into the canyon. Ignore all roads leading uphill out of the canyon. At just under one-half mile your trail changes to singletrack. Continue up the canyon. This is a great ride through this middle section—a singletrack trail, trees and bushes in an otherwise sagebrush covered landscape, no view of any reminders of man, much like being miles from the city. At 1 1/4 miles you will reach a mining area. Beginners should do a loop here and maybe do a little exploring. (Caution: Do not go inside mine shafts) The dumps (large yellowish mounds of dirt and rock) and shafts are the work of the Reno Mizpah Mine. Although the area has been extensively explored because of its proximity to the Reno-Sparks metro area, there are still bits of purple glass and other artifacts lying around.

To make a loop, at 1 1/4 miles, just prior to the first piles of yellow dirt, go left toward the pine trees. Swing right just before the trees to go across the corner of the mounded yellow dirt and resume following single track to the north. At 1 1/2 miles from your starting point on McCarran you will pass an adit (mine shaft opening) on your left and just above it reach a "T". The beginner loop requires that you turn right here, then take the next right to start back down the canyon. You will finish passing the yellow dumps at two miles and pass the wooden flume again at just under 3 miles. When you reach the parking area at McCarran you will have completed a total ride of 3 1/4 miles.

Intermediate and advanced riders have a number of options upon reaching the "T" just after the adit (1 1/2 miles from McCarran). Many riders turn left at the "T", then about 200 yards later when the road swings sharply left they go straight onto singletrack. This route crosses the road at two miles and again at just under 2 1/4 miles. At this second crossing it is possible to climb up to the flat (to the west) by staying on the singletrack (long, looping route that is at times obnoxiously rocky) or by turning right and following the road up and over. Either route will get you up onto a flat looking over to a north-south ridge with powerlines along it. From here many cyclists head for the radio towers (visible from the flat, just over the ridge to the right) that mark the top of Keystone Canyon (Ride 8). From there head south to McCarran. It is a little over 1 3/4 miles from the radio towers to McCarran, then after a one-half mile ride east you will be back to Rancho San Rafael Park. If you cover both canyons to make this intermediate/advanced loop, the ride will total from 6 1/2 to 7 miles, depending upon the route you use to get from one canyon to the other (the singletrack route is longer as well as more challenging).

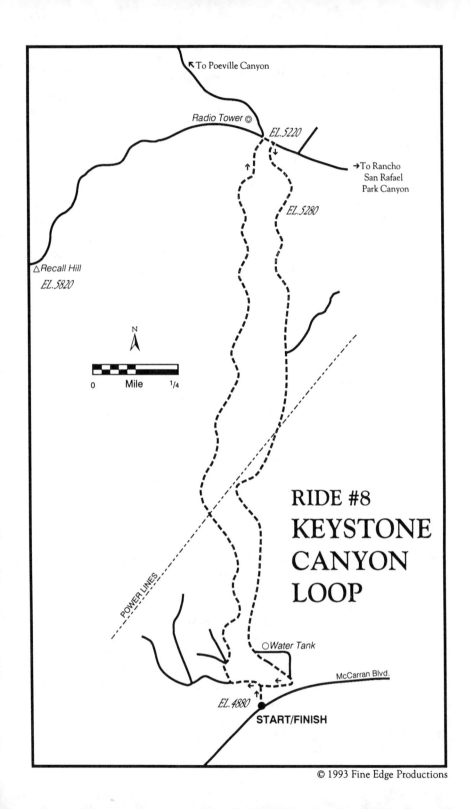

To Poeville Canyon

Radio Tower ◎

EL.5220

→To Rancho
San Rafael
Park Canyon

EL.5280

△*Recall Hill*
EL.5820

N

0   Mile   ¹⁄₄

POWER LINES

RIDE #8
KEYSTONE
CANYON
LOOP

○*Water Tank*

McCarran Blvd.

EL.4880

START/FINISH

© 1993 Fine Edge Productions

Ride #8
KEYSTONE CANYON LOOP

Difficulty: Intermediate
Distance: 3 3/4 miles
Starting Elevation: 4880 feet
Highest Elevation: 5280 feet
Map: USGS Reno 7.5

Trailhead

This ride, located in the southeastern foothills of Peavine Peak, is most commonly called Keystone Canyon, but dubbed by some as "Upper Canyon" (those using the latter name usually call Rancho San Rafael Park Canyon "Lower Canyon"). The name Keystone Canyon comes from the fact that the trailhead is located just east of the intersection of Keystone and McCarran. From downtown Reno, take Virginia Street north to McCarran, then turn left. Go west on McCarran to a point just past Keystone. Look for the parking area on the north side of McCarran, almost directly under a giant, light brown colored water storage tank.

Difficulty

This is a delightful ride up an interesting little canyon, and some of it in singletrack. The entire route, up and back, is only 3 3/4 miles long and has a total elevation gain of 400 feet if you take the high road loop back to McCarran (340 feet if you just turn around and come back down the canyon). With caution in a couple of rocky sections, this ride is suited to riders of all levels.

Description

From the parking area along McCarran, ride through the gate and follow the main road swinging to the left. After a few hundred feet you will encounter a fork—bear right, then turn right to go under powerlines (through here, if you look to the right you can see the canyon you are headed for). Stay on main road to drop into Keystone Canyon. Head up the canyon on the two-track jeep trail. At just over one-half mile you will simultaneously ride through the wash and under high powerlines. At three-fourths of a mile go straight ahead into the rocky wash (don't turn left to steep uphill).

At just under one mile you go through the wash and switch to singletrack. This section of the ride, three-fourths of a mile in length, is what has made Keystone Canyon popular—watch for high speed bike traffic coming the other way! Check out the interesting rock formations, and varieties of flora. At a little over 1 3/4 miles, back on two-track jeep trail, you will reach an area of radio towers. Just before you actually reach the first tower is a four-way intersection—here there are some choices to make.

For advanced or experts riders who like a challenge, try a side trip to the left. A left turn in front of the first tower starts a one-mile climb to the top of Recall Hill (an elevation gain of nearly 650 feet and some of it unrideable). This side trip is not recommended for beginners, but will provide the hardy with a fantastic view of the Truckee Meadows when they reach the top. For the adventurous, you can go west from the top, then downhill to the south and come out on McCarran about 1 1/2 miles west of Keystone. Another choice at the four-way intersection is to go straight ahead and by maintaining a northwesterly direction intersect with Poeville Canyon of Ride 9 (in this maze of jeep trails it's a little difficult to do it the first time you try)— once at Poeville Canyon you can climb up to the main Peavine Peak road or drop down to North Virginia Street (at Seneca in Horizon Hills).

For those not interested in exploring or in side trips, you must make a choice at the four-way intersection just before the radio towers. Either make a U-turn and go back down the canyon (a delightful downhilling experience, especially around banked corners) or turn right for an alternate route back to your starting point— the two routes back are the same distance (total ride of 3 3/4 miles), but the right turn adds a little climbing. To do the "loop", turn right at the four-way intersection, ride through the wash and up the little hill. Immediately past the fenceline turn right again and head uphill south, fol-

lowing the fenceline. Your road will swing away from the fence for a short distance (don't take roads to the left) and then back uphill to rejoin it. On your left through here is a large flat— directly to the east of it is Rancho San Rafael Park Canyon (Ride 20). At 2 3/4 miles from your starting point you will ride through a gate and shortly thereafter pass a small power station. Go past the power station and then bear right at the fork (stay along powerlines) at 3 miles. Follow the main road south, then down to the parking area along McCarran for a total mileage of 3 3/4 miles.

Ride #9 POEVILLE CANYON CLIMB

Difficulty: Intermediate
Distance: 5 1/2 miles
Starting Elevation: 5360 feet
Highest Elevation: 6380 feet
Map: USGS Reno/Verdi 7.5

Keystone Canyon singletrack.

Trailhead
This ride is located on the eastern flank of Peavine Peak. The trailhead is located at the southeast corner of the Horizon Hills housing development. To get to this starting point from downtown Reno, go north on Virginia Street, past McCarran and past Parr. At 4 1/2 miles from downtown turn left to stay on North Virginia (straight ahead leads to U.S. 395). A little over 2 1/2 miles from this turn, go left onto Seneca.

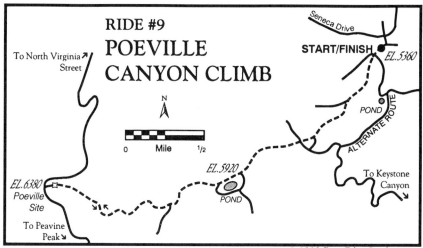

RIDE #9
POEVILLE CANYON CLIMB

To North Virginia Street

START/FINISH EL.5360

N

0   Mile   1/2

POND

EL.5920

EL.6380
Poeville Site

POND

To Keystone Canyon

To Peavine Peak

© 1993 Fine Edge Productions

Take Seneca for a little over one-half mile, then turn left on Kiowa Way. Follow Kiowa until the pavement ends (a few hundred feet) and the dirt parking area at that point is the Poeville Canyon Climb trailhead.

Difficulty

The ride to the Poeville site and back is not technically very difficult or very long, but it is relentlessly uphill. There is a 1000 foot elevation gain in the 2 3/4 miles from Kiowa to Poeville. In addition, there are dozens of side roads along the route begging for exploration— most of them are straight up the canyon walls or up numerous little side canyons. Because of the endurance/strength factor involved, the Poeville Canyon Climb is suited to intermediates or better.

Description

Poeville Canyon is probably the most interesting and prettiest of the Peavine canyons that lead into the Truckee Meadows. The history of the town of

Poeville and the Golden Fleece mine make it interesting, the ponds and the trees and bushes are dramatic in contrast to the nearby sage covered hills. To find Poeville Canyon, before you start riding, look to the southwest and you will see a jeep trail going up and over a nearby hill. From your starting point, turn right and go up that hill. At just over one-half mile bear left at the fork. At just over three-fourths of a mile you will encounter a four-way intersection— go straight ahead and drop down into Poeville Canyon. Head up the canyon (west).

At 1 1/2 miles you will reach a giant pond area— this man-made remnant of mining days long since past is a great place to explore. There are roads all around the pond and several leading up into the hills away from it. Spotted through this middle section of the Poeville Canyon Climb are thickets of trees and/or bushes, great places to rest, out of the sun on hot summer days. Continuing on up the canyon, you will ride through the wash at just over two miles, then swing right and continue climbing (don't take the road going up the little canyon to the left). Your destination is Poeville site, about three-fourths of a mile farther up the road. About all that is left are some trees and some mine dumps (mounds of dirt) from the Golden Fleece Mine. In the 1860's and 1870's there was a little mining camp located here, originally called Peavine. John Poe (reputed to be a cousin of Edgar Allan Poe) discovered gold and new names such as Poe City, Podunk, and Poeville were used. Poeville was the official name, at least for a while (1874 to 1878), because that was the name of the post office located there.

The Poeville site marks the turnaround point for the Poeville Canyon Climb. For those wishing to lengthen the ride, it is possible to go another few hundred feet (to the top of the canyon) and connect with the Peavine Peak road (Ride 11)— once connected, you can turn left and ride to the top of the mountain or turn right and ride all the way back down to Virginia Street (and then go south to get back to Horizon Hills).

For those simply riding Poeville Canyon out and back, after turning around at Poeville you will return to the big pond at just over four miles. At 4 3/4 miles you are back to the point where you dropped into the canyon. Here you can retrace the route that brought you to the canyon and end up back at Kiowa at just over 5 1/2 miles. Or for some variety in your return route, stay right and continue following Poeville Can-

yon to the east and then northeast. Stay with the canyon until you reach another, smaller pond— from just past this second pond go east and you will be back at your starting point. This alternate route, lengthening the part of the ride that stays in the canyon, adds another one-third mile to your total distance.

Ride #10 RING AROUND THE GOLF COURSE

Difficulty: Intermediate
Distance: 4 miles
Starting Elevation: 5220 feet
Highest Elevation: 5350 feet
Map: USGS Verdi 7.5

Trailhead
From downtown Reno, go north on Virginia Street, then turn left on McCarran. Take McCarran to Mae Anne and go west past the shopping center. Stay on Mae Anne Avenue, past Robb and Ambassador Drives. Turn right on Avenida De Landa, then left on Beaumont Parkway (follow signs to Northgate Golf Club). Don't turn left at Clubhouse Drive— keep on Beaumont until the pavement ends a few hundred feet later. Park just off the blacktop.

Difficulty
This ride is relatively short (4 miles), but involves several fairly steep climbs and descents, especially in the second half of the ride. Much of the trail (jeep

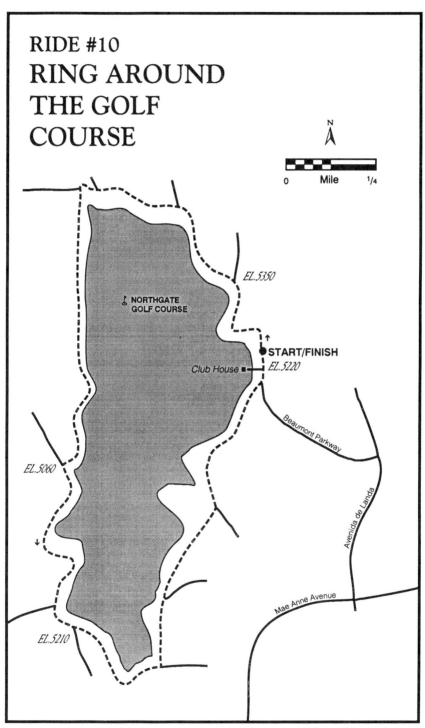

RIDE #10
RING AROUND
THE GOLF
COURSE

N

0   Mile   1/4

EL.5350

NORTHGATE
GOLF COURSE

START/FINISH
Club House   EL.5220

Beaumont Parkway

EL.5060

Avenida de Landa

EL.5210

Mae Anne Avenue

© 1993 Fine Edge Productions

roads and a little singletrack) is smooth and easy, but there are a few rocky and/or sandy areas to contend with. Ring Around the Golf Course is suited to intermediates or better riders.

Description

It would be difficult to get lost on this ride— just stay near the Northgate golf course, keeping it on your left as you completely go around it. Please be courteous to the golfers (don't make loud noises, don't ride right next to a green while they are putting, etc.) and do not go onto the course (it is fenced all around and is posted "No Trespassing"). Begin from the end of the Beaumont Parkway pavement by continuing uphill ahead (north). At one-quarter mile you will reach a fence corner— turn left which keeps you along the fenceline. At one-half mile stay left to continue along the golf course (the road to the right goes about 2 miles up into the Peavine Peak foothills). As you continue west along the north edge of the golf course, you have a great view of Peavine to your right. At three-fourths of a mile bear left at the fork, go briefly downhill, then turn left to stay near the golf course (you can see the fenceline up on the hill to your left).

At 1 1/3 miles from your starting point you will ride under powerlines— continue straight ahead on the main road (if you look ahead to the next hill, you can see where you will be soon). At 1 1/2 miles you will come right up to the fence, then swing right (west), then swing left (south). At just over 1 3/4 miles you reach a "T" at the bottom of the hill— bear left (south) to go up a steep hill and back to the golf course

fence. Continue on the main road, following the fenceline. At 2 1/4 miles the road swings south (left) at a fence corner and you will descend briefly. A few hundred feet later stay left at the fork (swing around another fence corner). The hill you will climb (the top is ahead to your right) is called Dark Mountain (elevation 5343). As you crest the hill (just over 2 1/2 miles), turn sharp left to head back toward the golf course.

As you are downhilling, you will encounter a fork at 2 3/4 miles (at a wrecked red vehicle). Bear left here and continue descending (right fork goes to MaeAnne). You will reach a "T" at the bottom of the hill (just under 3 miles)— turn left and go north. Don't turn right until you get to the golf course fence (3 1/4 miles). Go right directly in front of the fence to follow a two-rut jeep road up and over the hill. Once on top, then you have a steep downhill followed by a steep uphill (stay right alongside the fence). At 3 1/2 miles you will pass a fence corner as you are climbing (keep going straight, to the east). A few hundred feet after

Handbuilt rock fence.

the fence corner you will encounter a "T". Turn left, then go right along the fenceline. You will ride a singletrack in an easterly direction, down through one more little valley (stay along the fence). After this last climb you reach the pavement at the intersection of Clubhouse and Beaumont. Turn left to ride back to where you started for a total loop of four miles.

Ride #11
PEAVINE PEAK
CLIMB

Difficulty: Advanced
Distance: 14 miles
Starting Elevation: 5250 feet
Highest Elevation: 8266 feet
Map: USGS Verdi 7.5

Trailhead
Peavine Peak, named in the middle 1800's for wild peavines growing around areas of natural springs, is the mountain northwest of Reno— it is visible from most everywhere in the Truckee Meadows. There are two tops to this mountain, a few hundred yards apart, both just over 8250 feet in elevation. To get to the trailhead (the beginning of the Peavine Peak "service road"), go north on Virginia Street, past McCarran and Parr streets. At 4 1/2 miles from downtown turn left to stay on North Virginia (straight ahead leads to U.S. 395). A little over four miles after this turn and about 1/2 mile before a large green water storage tank, turn left onto a wide gravel road and park.

Difficulty
The difficulty in this ride is the long climb. As long as you don't get going too fast downhill, only modest technical skills are needed. This ride is rated as advanced or better because of the fitness requirement— you will gain over 3000 feet in elevation in the seven miles from Virginia Street to the top of the mountain.

Description
Head south on the wide gravel road, crossing railroad tracks just short of one-quarter mile. At one mile you will ride along powerlines. At a little over 1 1/2 miles you'll ride past mine tailings on your left. At 2 miles the tailings are on your right, and shortly after that the main road makes a U-turn left (straight ahead is gated and posted "No Trespassing"). At three miles you will be making a large left turn, around the head of a canyon— look down a few hundred feet and you will see some trees and the tailings from the "Golden Fleece Mine". Not much remains of the little mining camp called Poeville which was active here in the middle 1800's. Before 1863 this tiny settlement was called Peavine, but John Poe discovered a rich vein of gold and the names Poe City, Podunk, and Poeville were used. Poeville was the name of the post office there from September 1874 to March 1878. The road headed down the canyon through the Poeville site can be followed all the way back to the valley (Ride 9, coming out south of where you began this ride).

For the Peavine Peak Climb, continue ahead on the main road and at about 4 miles both peaks (and the expensive hardware atop them) come into view. At about 5 miles you will ride under power lines— some of the steepest climbing is through this section. You will soon encounter aspen trees along the left side of the road. You will see several roads headed off to the left prior to the last half-mile— these lead into a maze of jeep trails which can take you down to Mogul or Verdi, a little west of Reno. Continue on the main road and at about 6 miles you will leave the trees. At 6 3/4 miles you will have to choose which high point to ascend— they are very close in elevation and both afford fantastic views. After you have reached the top (or tops), you have ridden seven miles, and now you must turn around and descend back to the trailhead. There are two easily identified "alternate routes" (see the map), each about one mile long, to give you a little variety on the return trip. When you return to North Virginia Street you will have completed a total of 14 miles.

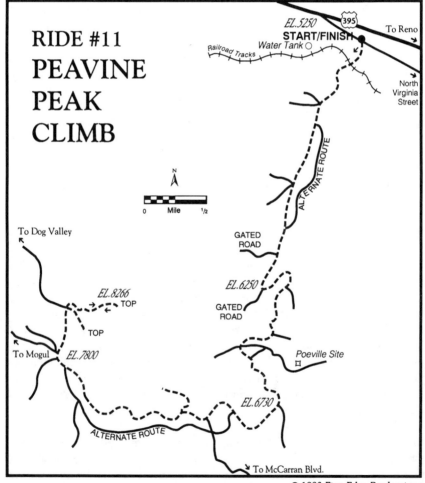

RIDE #11
PEAVINE
PEAK
CLIMB

EL.5250
395
To Reno
START/FINISH
Water Tank
Railroad Tracks
North Virginia Street

ALTERNATE ROUTE

N

0   Mile   1/2

To Dog Valley

GATED ROAD

EL.8266
TOP

EL.6250
GATED ROAD

TOP
To Mogul   EL.7800

Poeville Site

ALTERNATE ROUTE   EL.6730

To McCarran Blvd.

CHAPTER 3 RENO/SPARKS NORTHEAST

Ride #12 PahRah Range Loop; #13 Sparks Foothills Loop; #14 Pipeline Road; #15 Spanish Springs Canyon; #16 Desert Springs Loop; #17 Hungry Mountain Loop; #18 Truckee River Trail; #19 Mount Cavor Climb.

For cyclists who want to get away from the crowds, the high country of the Pah Rah Range— the low mountains east of Reno/Sparks and north of I-80 and the Truckee River— offers an austere beauty of its own. The routes in this area have the least usage by mountain bicyclists, and although the mountains are virtually treeless (even big shrubs or bushes are rare here) you can find quiet riding and great views here. Because of their low elevation and lack of shade and water, it's best to ride these mountains during fall, winter or spring and avoid hot summer afternoons.

Ride #12 PAH RAH RANGE LOOP

Difficulty: Expert
Distance: 9 1/4 miles
Starting Elevation: 4400 feet
Highest Elevation: 5570 feet
Map: USGS Vista 7.5

Trailhead
Despite its proximity to the Truckee Meadows, a high percentage of local residents cannot identify the Pah Rah Range. It is the group of mountains just north of the Truckee River (and I-80) and immediately east of Sparks. One of the range's low hills has a big white "S" on it. The name Pah Rah comes from "Pah-rah", the Shoshone word for river. To get to the starting point for this ride, take I-80 east from downtown Reno. Just prior to leaving the valley get off the freeway at the Vista Boulevard Exit. At Vista, turn left (north) and take the first right (across from Brierly Way) into the gravel pit. Park in the front of the pit, near Vista.

Difficulty
This ride is not long (under 10 miles) but offers extremes in mountain bike riding, both in ascending and descending and in obnoxiously rocky roads. Even the best of cyclists will likely find themselves walking at least short distances. The total elevation gain for the first two and one-half miles, the climb up into the Pah Rah highlands, is nearly 1200 feet, so endurance and strength are both tested during this ride!

Description
From your starting point, the front of the gravel pit at Vista and Brierly, go north through the pit (toward the freeway). Take the road swinging left and uphill. Stay on main road and you will encounter another pit at just over one-half mile (look for a badly rutted, rocky, steep little hill directly ahead of you as you approach the pit). After riding into

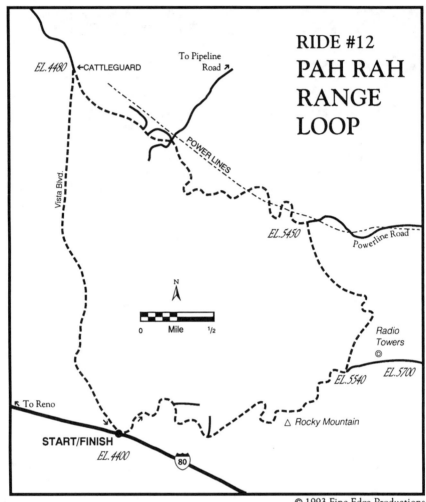

RIDE #12

PAH RAH RANGE LOOP

EL. 4480 ←CATTLEGUARD

To Pipeline Road ↗

POWER LINES

Vista Blvd.

EL. 5450

Powerline Road

N

0 Mile ½

Radio Towers ◎

EL. 5540 EL. 5700

To Reno

START/FINISH
EL. 4400

80

△ Rocky Mountain

© 1993 Fine Edge Productions

the pit, turn right, then left to go up the very steep little hill ("Impossible Hill"—impossible because I have never seen anyone ride all the way up it, despite the fact it is very short). At just under three-fourths of a mile (after you've gone under the powerlines), take the main road to the right and go up another steep little hill (not impossible, but tough). At the end of this short climb is a viewpoint, a fairly large flat area overlooking the valley. Stay

City view from the Pah Rah.

on the main road, continuing your climb.

At just over a mile, as your road is changing direction (from heading east to heading north) you will catch a glimpse of the Truckee River canyon and I-80. Immediately thereafter comes another short, steep climb. The mountain on your right through here is called Rocky (elevation 5598). The road swings right and shortly thereafter you will encounter a sharp switchback to the left near the top of Rocky (at just over 1 1/2 miles). Continue on this road until you reach a fork at 2 1/4. Your route goes left; however, bearing right will take you on an interesting side trip up to the top of an unnamed mountain with three radio towers on it (elevation 5700, a good place to take a break). If you go up to the towers and back it only adds three-quarters of a mile to the length of your ride.

Going left at the 2 1/4 mile fork provides the most relaxing portion of the mountainous part of the Pah Rah Range Loop. This section is relatively flat and the road surface is relatively smooth. At just over 3 3/4 miles you will encounter a "T" (powerline road)—turn left and begin your descent. At four miles you will ride under the powerlines and at 4 3/4 you go through a gate. Continue descending, staying on the main road. At 5 1/2 miles, just before a power pole, you encounter a four-way intersection— turn left, heading toward downtown Reno (in the distance). About 50 yards later bear right at the fork. About 300 yards later you will meet another fork and you can take either. The left route (toward trees)

and the right route (following powerlines) are approximately the same distance to where they rejoin at 6 1/2 miles (if you take the left fork, don't take roads turning sharp left at six miles; remember, you need to intersect the powerline road). At 6 1/2 miles go through the fence, then turn left across cattleguard to get to Vista Boulevard. Turn left on Vista and ride the pavement back to where you started near the freeway. Your total mileage for this loop into the Pah Rah Range is 9 1/4 miles (or exactly ten miles if you took the little side trip to the radio towers).

Ride #13
SPARKS FOOTHILLS LOOP

Difficulty: Beginner
Distance: 3 1/2 miles
Starting Elevation: 4480 feet
Highest Elevation: 4850 feet
Map: USGS Vista 7.5

Trialhead

From downtown Reno, take I-80 east. Leave the freeway at the last exit in the valley (Vista Boulevard), then turn left onto Vista. Just under three miles north of this turn and just before Pah Rah Park, turn right across the cattle guard. There is plenty of room to leave a vehicle here.

Difficulty

This ride is suited to cyclists of all skill levels. It is relatively short (3 1/2 miles) and does not require high level techni-

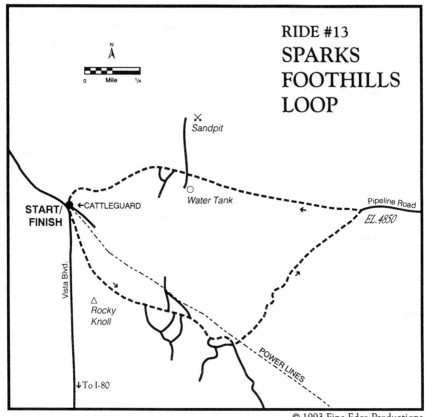

RIDE #13

SPARKS FOOTHILLS LOOP

Sandpit

N

0 Mile 1/4

START/ FINISH ←CATTLEGUARD

Water Tank

Pipeline Road

EL. 4850

Vista Blvd.

△ Rocky Knoll

POWER LINES

↓ To I-80

© 1993 Fine Edge Productions

cal skills. However, there is a little climbing, a little descending, and enough rocky and sandy sections to make it interesting.

Description

From the cattle guard go right (south) and through the opening in the fence. Immediately after going through the fenceline bear right (left would follow powerlines) and continue south parallel to Vista. At about one-third mile, just before a little rocky knoll, the road swings east. Towering directly ahead of you is the Pah Rah Range. Do not turn right on roads headed south around one-half mile— keep going east (to-

ward trees). You will pass the last tree (on your right), at just under three-fourths of a mile. At 3/4 mile you will ride through an open, sandy flat area (ignore all turning roads) and go ahead to the little uphill to the right of the powerlines. At one mile, near the top of the little hill, turn left toward the nearby power pole. Ignore the left turn just past the power pole and about 50 yards later you will reach a four-way intersection. Turn left here— the roads ahead go up into the mountains. After your left turn, you will encounter a modest climb, and will cross under the powerlines. You crest the hill at 1 1/3 miles— continue straight ahead. Follow the main road until you go through a fence to reach the "Pipeline Road" at two miles. To extend this ride, for a side trip consider turning right on Pipeline Road (Ride 14) and following it for a while (you can ride east on it for over 10 miles).

For cyclists not desiring any sidetrips, turn left (west) to get back to your starting point. Beginners should take care to not lose control on the very steep downhill immediately ahead. You will pass a giant water storage tank (on your left) at 2 3/4 miles. Stay on the main road headed west, back to your starting point— when you complete the loop as described herein, you will have ridden 3 1/2 miles.

Ride #14
PIPELINE ROAD

Difficulty: Expert
Distance: 26 miles
Starting Elevation: 4480 feet
Highest Elevation: 5420 feet
Map: USGS Vista/Patrick 7.5

Trailhead
From Virginia Street in downtown Reno, take I-80 east. Just prior to leaving the valley, get off the freeway at the Vista Boulevard Exit and turn left onto Vista. At about three miles north of I-80 (just before Pah Rah Park), turn right across the cattleguard— there is plenty of space here to leave vehicles. If you want to ride Pipeline Road only in one direction, the other end of this route may be reached by taking I-80 east of Reno/Sparks about 15 miles to

Tracy (Exit 32). Exit, go east one-fourth mile, then turn left under the freeway. Go another one-quarter mile to the cattleguard (near the loading corral)— this is the turnaround for the 26-mile out and back ride— if you leave a vehicle here you will only have to ride one direction (13 miles).

Difficulty
Pipeline Road, when done as an out and back, is best suited to experts. If you arrange a shuttle so as to have to ride only one way, it is still nearly an expert ride!

Description
This ride allows an extended escape into the Pah Rah Range adjacent to the Truckee Meadows. For much of it, cyclists will see few signs of the city they left below— this is a great "get-away" ride. A gas pipe was recently entrenched, from Sparks to Tracy (13 miles east), and this ride follows that pipeline. Unlike typical roads (that must take into account steepness of grade to assure that cars or trucks can negotiate them) this one does not traverse sidehills or wind around to go up and over the mountains. A pipe and the road alongside it are pretty much routed "as the crow flies". Consequently, this route from the Truckee Meadows up into the Pah Rah Range and exiting into the Truckee River canyon 13 miles later is a roller coaster ride— it includes long, grueling sections where you are either headed straight up a hill or straight down the other side. Pipeline Road cuts a wide swath, ranging from 20 to 50 feet, and much of it is relatively smooth (by desert jeep road standards). Also, when

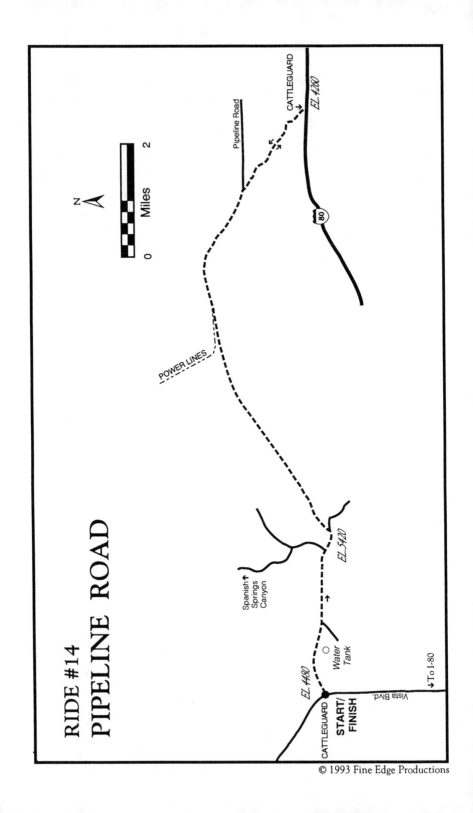

RIDE #14
PIPELINE ROAD

N

0   Miles   2

CATTLEGUARD

EL. 4260

Pipeline Road

80

POWER LINES

Spanish
Springs
Canyon

EL. 5420

Water
Tank

EL. 4480

CATTLEGUARD

START/
FINISH

Vista Blvd.

↓To I-80

© 1993 Fine Edge Productions

confronted by extremely steep hills, there often is a road around them (put in so work vehicles could safely go through)— although they lengthen your route a little, they will ease the climb in some of the most strenuous sections.

From your starting point, the cattleguard next to Vista, go straight ahead (east). At nearly one-half mile bear right to stay along the powerlines and continue east. At just over three-fourths of a mile the powerlines end (there is a water tank to your right)— go straight ahead, continuing east, up a very steep hill.

At 1 1/2 miles you will pass a road through a fenceline on your right (see Ride 13). At three miles you will crest a hill after a long tough climb (to 5420 feet elevation). If you pause here, turn around and check out the great panoramic view of the Truckee Meadows and the mountains to the west. From this point your route will be mostly headed northeast— just continue following the wide swath cut by the pipeline work crew. At 4 1/2 miles you will go downhill into a large flat. Enjoy a mile-long stretch of wide, smooth road with no climbing or descending!

At 7 1/4 miles you will reach the powerlines— bear right and continue following pipeline road (in a generally eastward direction). There is a very steep, short, white-colored hill to climb at nine miles (this is one of several little hills with an optional road around, if you want to avoid them). At 9 1/2 miles you will pass under powerlines.

When you reach the flat at 11 miles (nearly down to the canyon floor's elevation of 4260 feet), the powerlines you have been following make a right turn— here you also turn right and leave the pipeline road. A few hundred feet later, at a "T", turn left and follow the main road (southeast) down to the freeway. After riding under powerlines several times, go through the fenceline at just under 12 1/2 miles. Just past the loading corral, the turnaround for an out and back ride is the cattleguard at 13 miles. When you follow the pipeline road all the way back to the cattleguard next to Vista Boulevard, you will have completed a total ride of 26 miles.

Ride #15
SPANISH SPRINGS CANYON

Difficulty: Advanced
Distance: 16 miles
Starting Elevation: 4470 feet
Highest Elevation: 5220
Map: USGS Vista 7.5

Trailhead
From downtown Reno go north on Virginia to McCarran Boulevard and turn right. Follow McCarran to northeast Sparks (where McCarran swings south), then turn onto Baring Boulevard. Go east, past Reed High School, until Baring ends (a "T") and turn left onto Vista Boulevard. Follow Vista until the pavement ends (just past Los

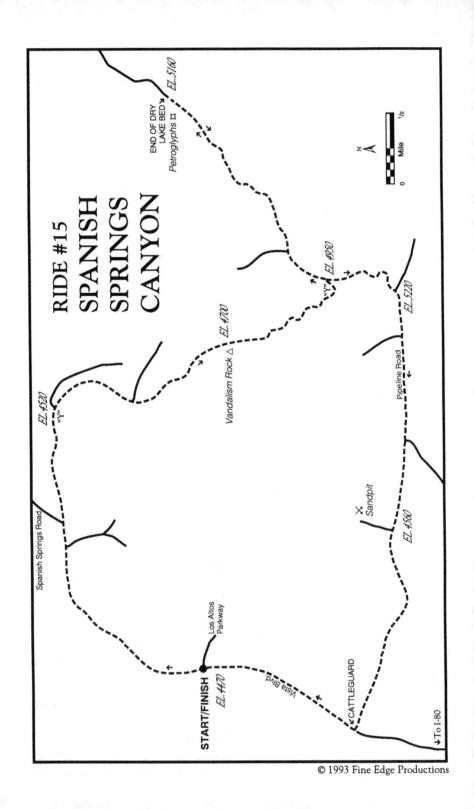

RIDE #15
SPANISH SPRINGS CANYON

EL. 5160

END OF DRY
LAKE BED
Petroglyphs ⌷

EL. 4950
"Y"

EL. 5220

Pipeline Road

Vandalism Rock △ EL. 4700

EL. 4520
"Y"

Sandpit
✕

EL. 4560

Spanish Springs Road

Los Altos
Parkway

START/FINISH
EL. 4470

Vista Blvd.

CATTLEGUARD

↓ To I-80

N

0   Mile   ½

© 1993 Fine Edge Productions

Altos Parkway). There is room to park on the right.

Difficulty

This ride is suited to advanced mountain bikers and above. It is not extraordinarily long (16 miles) but involves some steep and rocky ascents and descents. There are a couple of hills where only very strong riders can avoid getting off their bikes and walking.

Description

Around the turn of the century local landowners dubbed an area of natural springs in the Pah Rah Range "Spanish", because they were frequented by Mexican squatters. Today, Spanish Springs Canyon and the dry lake beds above it give cyclists a feeling of the Nevada "outback" even though they are actually very close to town. For much of the ride you cannot see any signs of the nearby urban population (other than the inevitable litter along the road). From Los Altos Parkway head north on Vista. After about 1 1/2 miles you will swing to the right and head due east. At 2 1/4 miles the main road turns left to the north, but you will go straight ahead on a wide dirt road. Ride on this road until you reach a "Y" at 3 1/2 miles— proceed on the smaller road, the right fork. Follow this road south, to the mouth of Spanish Springs Canyon, ignoring little roads to the right and left.

At 5 1/2 miles from where you started you'll see Vandalism Rock, a large boulder on your right with white paint reading "Bud Loop". Continue ahead, gently climb on up the canyon.

Near the end of this box canyon there is an intersection, a "Y" (at almost 6 1/2 miles). You must turn left here and ride up the steep hill to the top (it is possible to shorten your total ride to 12 miles by turning right here, but you will miss the very interesting dry lake area). After the climb follow the main road down along the edge of the large dry lake bed. The lake bed is identified by rounded black lava rocks strewn all over soft sand/silt— it calls to mind a lunarscape. At 8 1/2 miles the lake bed ends. At this point look uphill to your left; the very large rock outcropping on the hillside has some interesting Native American petroglyph art. These carvings include several bighorn sheep and rattlesnakes, and are estimated to be about 3000 years old. Please do not disturb them! And if you see anyone vandalizing them (it is illegal, as well as immoral, to disturb them and the penalties are substantial), please report it to the Washoe County Sheriff. Pause here for a rest break and hike up the hill to see fascinating prehistoric rock art.

After your break, turn around and return the two miles back to the intersec-

High desert wild mustangs.

tion at the top of Spanish Springs Canyon (10.5 miles). Go left at this intersection and soon you will climb another steep hill. Up on top as you go past a road coming from the left a view of the Truckee Meadows will appear (11 1/4 miles). Head downhill, following the main road to the west— you have merged with Pipeline Road (Ride 14). There is a right turn to a large sandpit at 13 miles (you will continue straight ahead). This intersection marks the base of a very steep hill. Proceed ahead (west), following the power lines to Vista (14 miles). Turn right onto Vista Boulevard and ride the shoulder for two miles to return to where you started (16 miles total riding).

Ride #16
DESERT
SPRINGS LOOP

Difficulty: Intermediate
Distance: 5 miles
Starting Elevation: 4520 feet
Highest Elevation: 5080 feet
Map: USGS Griffith Canyon/Reno NE 7.5

Trailhead

To reach the starting point for this ride, take Virginia Street north from downtown. Just past the University of Nevada campus, turn right on McCarran and go east for four miles. Turn left onto Pyramid Way (which becomes Pyramid Highway) and go 5 1/2 miles north. Watch for the Desert Springs subdivision sign and turn left onto Dolores. Follow Dolores for just over one-half mile (past Robert Banks Boulevard) to where the pavement ends. There is plenty of room in this area to park vehicles.

Difficulty

This ride is not long (5 miles) but has sufficiently rough and sandy sections and a modest climb to warrant an intermediate designation. Taken leisurely and carefully, many beginners would also find this ride enjoyable. For advanced or expert mountain bikers there are some opportunities for tough uphill sidetrips (on several old mining roads) to lengthen and toughen the Desert Springs Loop.

Description

Take the main dirt road to the right (north). Identify the large water tank in the distance to the north— you will head generally toward it for the first 1 1/2 miles of this ride. At just under one-half mile, continue ahead through a multi-road intersection (make note of this area as it is where the loop portion of this ride begins and ends). Go through several four-way intersections— the roads to the left and right for the four-way at almost exactly one mile are in a wash. At 1 1/2 miles watch for a left turn in which you can see the road going up to the base of the mountain. If you find yourself riding in a wash or encountering a paved highway, you missed the proper turn.

After your left turn, you will climb steadily west for almost a mile. The cedars and pines through here make the ride very pleasant. At just under two miles ignore the turn to the left (south). At just under 2 1/2 miles you

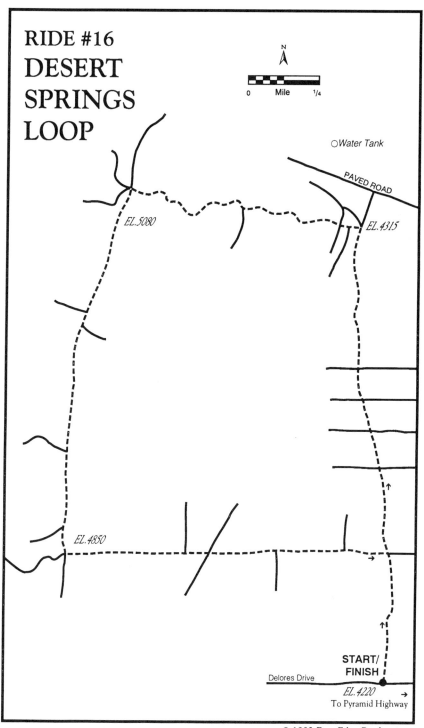

RIDE #16
DESERT
SPRINGS
LOOP

N

0   Mile   1/4

○Water Tank

PAVED ROAD

EL.5080

EL.4315

EL.4850

START/
FINISH

Delores Drive

EL.4220
To Pyramid Highway

will encounter a four way intersection. Turn left and head downhill to the south (straight ahead goes uphill, then turns sharp right in about 100 yards). There are some great views here. At 2 1/2 miles bear left at the "Y" (right offers some exploration opportunities). At 2 3/4 miles is another exploration road to the mining areas on your right—continue ahead south. A few hundred feet later you will pass a road to the left (it goes all the way down to the flat). Go past another road to the right around 3 3/4 miles. A few hundred feet later you will encounter a four-way intersection— turn left to ride downhill to intersect your original road.

Go east, ignoring turns, to just over 4 1/2 miles. In an open flat area you will encounter your original road, ending the loop portion of the Desert Springs Loop ride. Turn right and head south to return to where you started. When you reach the pavement at Dolores, you will have completed slightly over five miles.

Ride #17 HUNGRY MOUNTAIN LOOP

Difficulty: Intermediate
Distance: 14 3/4 miles
Starting Elevation: 5050 feet
Highest Elevation: 5525 feet
Map: USGS Reno NE 7.5

Trailhead

This ride begins in an area a few miles north of Reno called Lemmon Valley. From downtown, take Virginia Street and U.S. 395 north to Exit 74 (Lemmon Drive). Follow Lemmon Drive to Idaho Street (just past Arizona, about 5 miles from 395). Turn right and go one and one-half miles to a stop sign (Oregon). Turn right and go one-quarter mile, then turn left onto Matterhorn Boulevard (another stop sign). Just ahead the blacktop ends and the Hungry Mountain Loop starts there. Park your vehicle just beyond the paved road.

Difficulty

If you do this ride in a leisurely fashion, most intermediates will find it within their capabilities. There are some rocky and some very soft/sandy sections to provide a modest technical challenge. For the most part, the climbing is on gentle grade. Advanced and expert riders will enjoy a fast-paced run on this loop.

Description

This is an interesting ride which includes a long run up an unnamed canyon, a ride up and over Hungry Mountain pass, a flat section along the edge of Hungry Valley, and some pedaling in Lemmon Valley. Much of the ride is out of sight of houses and other signs of civilization, and there are sections of the route in a desert forest.

From your parking place, go straight ahead (north) on the wide dirt road (past the mail boxes). At just over one mile, ignore the road to the right—continue climbing on the main road. Cresting the hill, at 2 1/4 miles, you will pass a sign on your right saying "Community of Christ, Consecrated

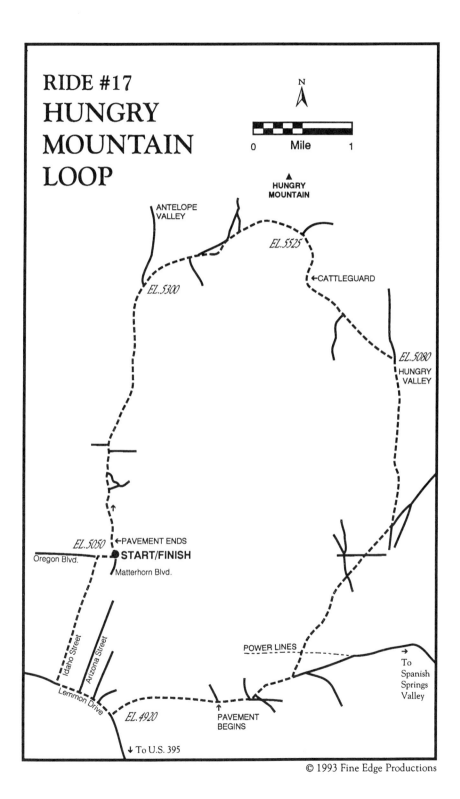

RIDE #17
HUNGRY
MOUNTAIN
LOOP

N

0   Mile   1

▲
HUNGRY
MOUNTAIN

ANTELOPE
VALLEY

EL.5525

←CATTLEGUARD

EL.5300

EL.5080
HUNGRY
VALLEY

EL.5050
Oregon Blvd.   ←PAVEMENT ENDS
● START/FINISH
Matterhorn Blvd.

Idaho Street   Arizona Street

POWER LINES   →
To
Spanish
Springs
Valley

Lemmon Drive

EL.4920   PAVEMENT
BEGINS

↓ To U.S. 395

Sanctuary". Now, as you head downhill, you can see a large valley ahead (Antelope Valley).

At just under three miles, just past another Community of Christ sign, take the road to the right (turn along the fenceline). At 3 1/2 miles you will pass another gated entry to the Sanctuary on your right— ride straight ahead. At four miles continue ahead on the main road (ignore road to the left). Around 4 1/2 miles the climb steepens as you ride through a burn area.

At five miles you will crest Hungry Mountain pass (5525 feet in elevation). Through this high flat area, don't turn— continue ahead (southeast) on a winding little road. At just under 5 1/2 miles go straight ahead across the cattleguard and follow the main road southeast, down toward Hungry Valley. Through here and ahead you will encounter numerous sections with very soft sand. At just under six miles, ignore the road to the right and the singletrack to the left. Just past two rusty tanks on your right, bear right at the "T"— this turn is at just over 6 1/2 miles and routes you south along the edge of the valley.

At just over 8 1/4 miles bear right at the four-way intersection; you will now be heading southwest (toward Peavine Peak in the distance). One-half mile later, continue straight at another four-way intersection. At ten miles, continue ahead (southwest) and pass under the powerlines.

At just over 10 1/4 miles bear right at the "T" (a left turn here will take you east, then southeast, through the hills to Spanish Springs Valley).

You will encounter pavement around 11 miles. Continue ahead, but move a few feet to the right up onto the singletrack/footpath that runs alongside the blacktop road. At just under 12 1/2 miles turn right onto the paved bike trail that parallels Lemmon Drive. From this point, you will follow the same route you drove to get to the starting point for this ride. Turn right onto Idaho at 13 miles, then turn right onto Oregon at the stop sign (just under 14 1/2 miles). One-quarter mile ahead turn left onto Matterhorn and just ahead is the end of the paved road where you started (for a total mileage of just over 14 3/4 miles).

Ride #18
TRUCKEE
RIVER TRAIL

Difficulty: Beginner
Distance: 13 miles
Starting Elevation: 4460 feet
Highest Elevation: 4460 feet
Map: USGS Reno/Vista 7.5

Trailhead

From downtown, turn east on 2nd Street (between Harrahs and Cal-Neva casinos). Go past Kirman and turn left on Manuel, then left on Kuenzli. Just prior to the Reno Gazette Journal building is a short paved bicycle path down to the river where you turn right onto the Truckee River Trail. Park alongside the paved path, near Kuenzli.

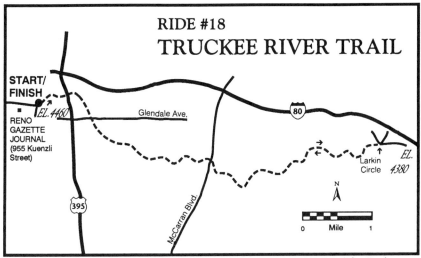

RIDE #18
TRUCKEE RIVER TRAIL

START/
FINISH

EL. 4460

RENO
GAZETTE
JOURNAL
(955 Kuenzli
Street)

Glendale Ave.

80

Larkin
Circle

EL. 4380

N

McCarran Blvd.

395

0   Mile   1

© 1993 Fine Edge Productions

Difficulty

This is an easy ride, on an almost flat (elevation varies from 4380 to 4460 feet) paved trail, suited to riders of all skill levels. It also can be ridden by cyclists with road bikes, but periodic bumpiness and numerous joggers, walkers, dogs, and so on, can prove frustrating if you are in a hurry. This is the most heavily used of all the bike trails in the Reno-Carson City area.

Description

This trail is a public project to provide extended river access, a place for people to enjoy the natural beauty of the Truckee. The river was named in the mid-1840's by a party of explorers from Iowa who were assisted by a Paiute Indian guide named Truckee— the word Truckee means "all right" or "very well". The Truckee River Trail is a paved path following the river from west of downtown all the way to a point east of Sparks. The section described herein allows a pleasant, almost flat,

Hammering uphill.

non-stop aerobic ride for 6 1/2 miles (one way). You will cross the river on a small bridge, ride through several small parks, and pass countless rocky riffles in the river. Always be alert for other recreationists (and their dogs). The trail ends at Larkin Circle (near I-80) in Sparks— typically, cyclists turn around here and ride the trail west back to their vehicles (13 miles total). You will see mileage markers during your ride. If you start where this description indicates (next to the Reno Gazette Journal building), after two miles you will pass a sign saying "1 mile". At the end of the paved trail when you've completed 6 1/2 miles the sign says "5.5 miles". For cyclists without odometers, these markers are helpful in gauging distances.

RIDE #19 MOUNT CAVOR CLIMB

Difficulty: Expert
Distance: 6 miles
Starting Elevation: 4480 feet
Highest Elevation: 5940 feet
Map: USGS Vista 7.5

Trailhead

This ride begins just off the freeway (I-80) nearly 10 miles east of downtown Reno. From Virginia Street, just north of the casinos, take I-80 east. Leave the freeway at the Mustang Exit (#23). At the stop sign, go left under the freeway (a right turn here will take you to Nevada's most famous legal brothel!). Just through the underpass, turn left (at another stop sign). Don't get back on the freeway— go straight ahead. Park in the first area with wide shoulders (its just before passing under powerlines).

Difficulty

This ride is an excellent test of strength and endurance. If you are not sure if you are an "expert" rider, try this one. Strong riders can pedal the three mile climb without resting or walking.

The complete six mile ride consists of three miles uphill (with almost 500 feet of elevation gain per mile) and three miles downhill. Significant technical skills are not in demand as most of the road is relatively smooth, but there are sheer drops alongside much of the route so caution in downhilling is important. There are places where losing control at high speed could send a rider tumbling several hundred feet down a rocky sidehill!

Description

This ride follows a road from the Truckee River Canyon to the top of Mount Cavor in the Pah Rah Range. The road is kept in good repair as it provides access to electronic equipment on the top of the mountain. From your parking area just off the freeway, start ahead (uphill) passing under the powerlines. At just over one-quarter mile you will encounter a "Y"— bear right onto the dirt road (the left is paved). Stay on the main road through the lower pit area.

At just over three-fourths of a mile the road swings left. Just as you finish the turn make a sharp right turn and head

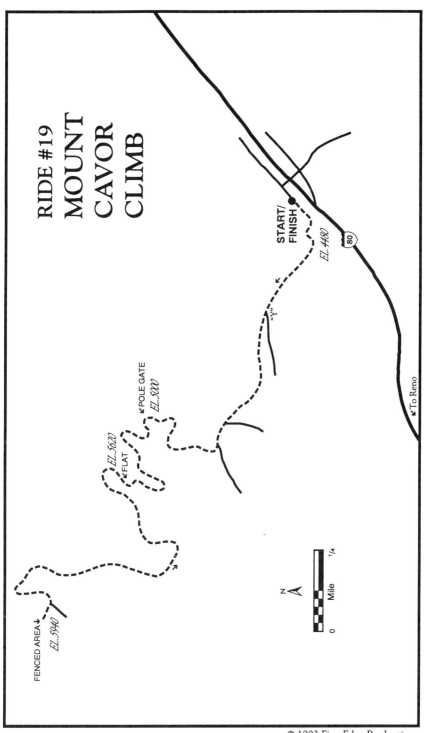

RIDE #19
MOUNT
CAVOR
CLIMB

START/
FINISH

EL. 4480

80

←To Reno

"Y"

POLE GATE
EL. 5000

EL. 5620
FLAT

FENCED AREA→
EL. 5940

N

Mile

0   1/4

uphill (if you don't turn, you'll ride into the pit ahead). From this point, there are no turn options— just follow the road to the top. At just over 1 1/4 miles you will pass a pole gate (the elevation here is 5000 feet, one-third of the climb). As you continue ascending, you will encounter increasingly panoramic views. After just over 2 1/4 miles you will ride through a short flat section where the road swings from the western slope of Cavor to the east. The flat is easy to identify because more than one-half mile before and after it is a relentless uphill grade. The flat is at 5620 feet, so as you come around the hill approaching it you have completed two-thirds of your climb.

From the brief flat, continue your ascent to the top. When cresting, there is a "Y"— head right to the highest point. The turnaround place for this ride is the gate to the fenced area on top. It has a sign that says "U.S. Property, No Trespassing". Stay clear of the fenced area (there are safety hazards created by the microwave/electronic equipment). Turn around and ride/coast downhill. Make certain that you descend in control— there are steep, long drops around the outside of most turns. The descent is sufficiently steep that it is possible to attain very high speeds, so check your brakes before heading down to assure stopping power when you need it. When you reach the parking area just off the freeway, you will have completed a six mile out and back ride.

Toll Road Historical Marker.

 RENO/SPARKS NORTHEAST

Ride #20 Toll Road Climb; #21 Mira Loma Road; #22 Virginia Mountains in the Valley; #23 Lagomarsino Petroglyphs; #24 Barrel Springs Road; #25 Long Valley Loop; #26 Lockwood to Washington; #27 Panorama Point; #28 Dry Lake Loop; #29 Sixmile Canyon.

Many cyclists consider the Virginia Range— the mountains south and east of Reno, Sparks and Washoe Valley— the most interesting area for riding, especially in terms of history. The region also offers the most miles of jeep trails for exploring. Nestled high in the range, Virginia City, the old mining town established in 1859, is now a national historic landmark. At its peak, it was the richest mining town in the world— a boisterous 24-hour town of over 30,000 residents— that produced more than $400 million in silver and gold in a few short years. For many miles around, you can still find remnants of Virginia City's heyday. Consider a ride or drive to check out the town and its history before you cycle the surrounding hills and valleys.

Ride #20 TOLL ROAD CLIMB

Difficulty: Advanced
Distance: 12 miles
Starting Elevation: 4515 feet
Highest Elevation: 6360 feet
Map: USGS Steamboat/Virginia City 7.5

Trailhead
Heading south from Reno on U.S. 395 drive 10 miles to the Mt. Rose junction and turn left on Highway 341 toward Virginia City. After one-half mile, Toll Road will angle off to the right— there is plenty of parking near this intersection.

Difficulty
Much of this ride is an extended, mod- erately steep, but minimally technical hill climb. The entire trip features an 1800 foot gain in elevation, most of it concentrated in the last four miles of the six-mile long climb. Going up takes about an hour and the return trip about half of that. The Toll Road Climb is best suited to advanced or better riders.

Description
Toll Road is the "old road to Virginia City". Most traffic going to the historic old mining town now uses Highway 341 (Geiger Grade). This climb uti- lizes the original, unpaved Geiger Grade, built by a Mr. Geiger who ran a tollhouse at the top of it in 1861 and 1862. During the Comstock mining days, this road carried a tremendous amount of traffic, and according to old Virginia City newspapers, stagecoach holdups were ordinary occurrences.

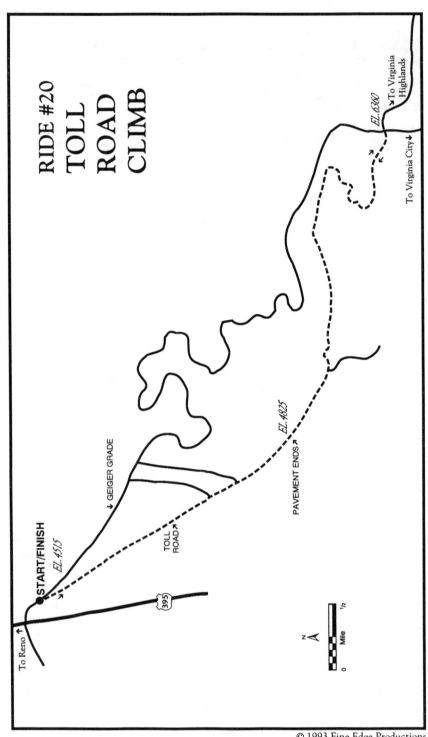

RIDE #20
TOLL
ROAD
CLIMB

To Reno ↑

START/FINISH
EL. 4515

↓ GEIGER GRADE

TOLL
ROAD ↗

EL. 4825

PAVEMENT ENDS ↗

EL. 6360

↘ To Virginia
Highlands

To Virginia City ↓

395

N
↑

0   Mile   ½

© 1993 Fine Edge Productions

The first third of the Toll Road Climb, starting near Highway 341, is on pavement through a residential neighborhood. As you ride on, after two miles the pavement ends and the road will get increasingly steep. For the four-mile climb on dirt, you will follow very picturesque canyons, an area of high desert dotted with cedars and pines. At about 4 1/2 miles do not take the road going sharply left. At five miles you will encounter a brief fence line as you swing around a curve to the left. The ride is arduous (especially near the end), but much more peaceful and scenic for mountain biking than nearby Geiger Grade. The Toll Road climb ends when you intersect the main highway. At this point you should have a car waiting if you are done riding. Otherwise, you have the option of descending back down to the Truckee Meadows by either Geiger Grade (7 miles) or Toll Road (out and back total of 12 miles). If you have plenty of time, consider a side trip to Virginia City (a few miles to the south).

Ride #21
MIRA LOMA
ROAD

Difficulty: Beginner
Distance: 10 miles
Starting Elevation: 4580 feet
Highest Elevation: 4580 feet
Map: USGS Steamboat 7.5

Trailhead
From central Reno take Virginia Street ten miles south to the Mt. Rose junction. Turn left onto Geiger Grade (headed toward Virginia City)— after three-fourths of a mile turn left onto Mira Loma Road and go to the parking lot at Brown School (Mira Loma and Reading).

Difficulty
This ride is for the most part very flat (elevation varies from 4420 to 4580 feet), and out and back totals only 10 miles. There are a few short sections that are a little rocky and a couple of places with loose sand— otherwise the ride requires very little technical riding ability. This Virginia Foothills to Hidden Valley ride (excluding the various side trips that are possible) is suitable for riders of all skill levels.

Description
Beginning at Brown School, ride north on Mira Loma Road. After one mile, as you pass the quarry on the right, the pavement ends. Follow the main road as it swings right and goes briefly downhill. Travel the wide gravel road, headed north, along the ranchlands/wetlands. The view from here extends to downtown Reno, Peavine Mountain, and to the Carson Range to the west. At 2 3/4 miles the main road swings right (into the parking lot for a gun club)— you should go straight (on to a smaller, more primitive road), continuing along the fence line (on your left).

At four miles there is a power station a little up the hill to the right. If you would like a side trip, there is a road to the right up to the power station. Beyond that you can swing right at the power station to follow a road up through an interesting little canyon

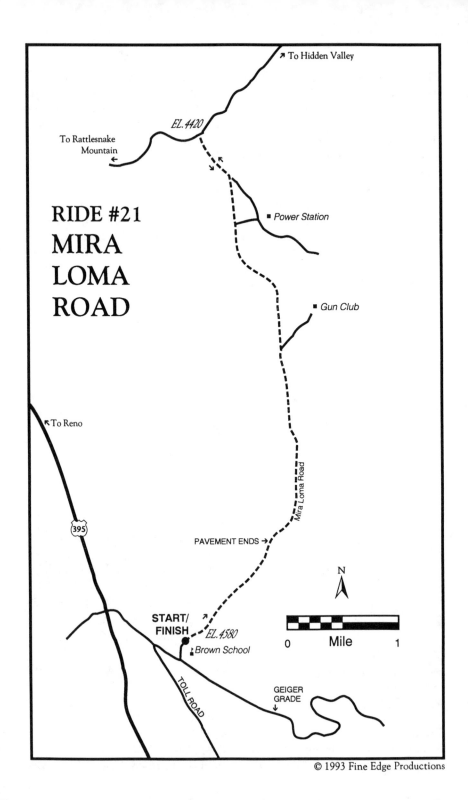

RIDE #21
MIRA
LOMA
ROAD

To Hidden Valley

EL. 4420

To Rattlesnake
Mountain

Power Station

Gun Club

To Reno

395

Mira Loma Road

PAVEMENT ENDS →

N

START/
FINISH

EL. 4580

Brown School

Mile

0   1

GEIGER
GRADE
↓

TOLL ROAD

© 1993 Fine Edge Productions

(and clear up and over to Virginia City if you choose). If you are not making a side trip continue north on Mira Loma Road. At five miles you reach a "T"— this turnaround point (directly back to Brown School, with no sidetrips, will give you a total distance of 10 miles). For additional side trips from the "T" you can (a) go to the left, through a large yellow steel gate and ride all the way up to the top of Rattlesnake Mountain, or (b) turn right and ride up and over the hill into the Hidden Valley subdivision.

Ride #22
VIRGINIA MOUNTAINS TO THE VALLEY

Difficulty: Intermediate
Distance: 13 1/2 miles
Starting Elevation: 5790 feet
Highest Elevation: 5960 feet
Map: USGS Steamboat 7.5

Trailhead
Heading south from Reno on U.S. 395, drive 10 miles to the Mt. Rose junction and turn left onto Highway 341 toward Virginia City. Climb Geiger Grade (341) up to the Virginia Highlands turnoff (about 7 miles)— turn left onto Cartwright Road. Follow Cartwright a little over 3 miles to its junction with Lousetown Road (watch for the fire station). There is plenty of parking near this intersection. Unless you want to ride a long and arduous loop (described later) or to backtrack the ride outlined herein (also difficult), you need to have a car waiting for you at the power station near Mira Loma (8 1/2 mile ride) or at the intersection of Mira Loma and Highway 341 (just over 13 1/2 miles).

Difficulty
This ride, the fire station to Highway 341, is best suited to intermediate or better cyclists. The climbs, except for one short steep portion near the top, are relatively easy. The difficulty is in the descent— it is long and sometimes steep and rocky. There are repeated possibilities for novice riders to lose control and crash. If you choose to cycle Virginia Mountains to the Valley (to Highway 341) as an out and back (27 miles), then it becomes an expert ride (double the distance and considerably steeper climbing)— when going back to the fire station you will climb from 4420 feet (power station) to 5960 in just a few miles!

Downhill run.

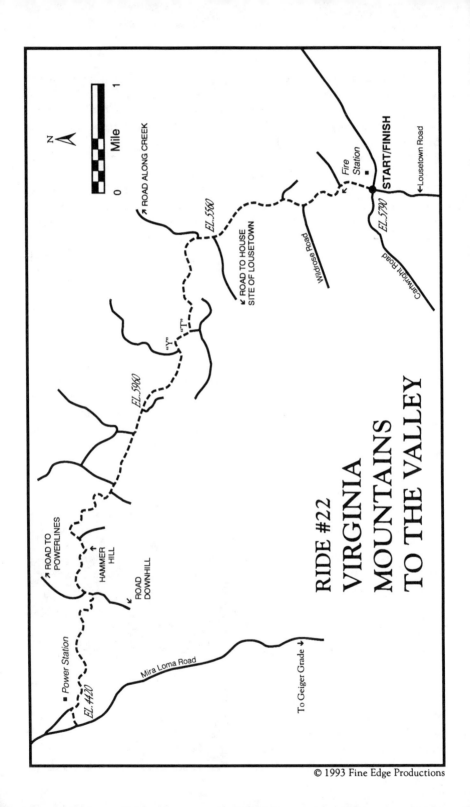

RIDE #22
VIRGINIA
MOUNTAINS
TO THE VALLEY

START/FINISH

Fire Station

← Lousetown Road

Cammisihi Road

Wildrose Road

← ROAD TO HOUSE SITE OF LOUSETOWN

EL. 5790

EL. 5560

↑ ROAD ALONG CREEK

N

0   Mile   1

EL. 5960

"T"

↑ ROAD TO POWERLINES

HAMMER HILL

ROAD DOWNHILL

Power Station

EL. 4420

Mira Loma Road

To Geiger Grade →

Description

The Virginia Mountains offer an interesting and very scenic high desert ride. The mountain range and Virginia City were named after "Old Virginia" Fennimore, a prospector who lived and worked around the Comstock in the 1850's. You will ride in sagebrush covered hills dotted with cedars and pines—interesting and beautiful high desert terrain. There are herds of wild horses roaming the highlands, as well as numerous other animals and birds. The run begins at the intersection of Cartwright Road and Lousetown Road (next to the fire station). Head north on Lousetown Road and you'll pass Panamint (just over one-quarter mile), Wildrose (just over three-quarters of a mile) and Bull Frog (1 mile). Two miles from Cartwright Road and after crossing the creek bed twice, a network of roads appears ahead (including one to a house in the canyon to the west). This is the site of "Lousetown", a small burg populated by thieves and scoundrels during Virginia City's heyday (middle 1800's). Apparently, this settlement was originally called Louisetown, but due to the nature of the folks who populated it, the name was changed. Very little indication of the dozens of buildings and the racetrack that used to be there can be found today.

Avoid roads to the left and the low road to the right which continues along Lousetown Creek. Just to the left of that creekside road you can see one headed gently up the hillside— this begins the two mile, mostly gradual climb to the flats up high in the Virginia Mountain Range. At 3 1/2 miles you'll encounter a "T"; turn right and continue to a "Y" (3 3/4 miles) where you turn left. The crest is just over four miles from the fire station and offers your first view of downtown Reno. This begins several miles of panoramic views of the Truckee Meadows with a high mountain (Carson Range) backdrop. Continue ahead, staying on the main road, ignoring left and right turns. At about six miles the descent steepens, and about one-half mile later you'll encounter Hammer Hill— this is a short little "up one side and down the other" hill. After you carefully go down the backside of the hill, for a challenge turn around at the lone tree and try to ride back up! Continue on, ignoring side roads (mostly headed up to power lines). At about 7 1/4 miles there is a four-way intersection— do not take the road to the left headed downhill or the one to the right uphill to the power poles. You want the road that goes straight very briefly then curls around the hillside to the right. Stay on the main road, descending to the power station (8 1/2 miles) back in the valley. To get to Highway 341, turn left in front of the power station, go one-fourth mile to Mira Loma, turn left and follow it for 4 3/4 miles to Geiger Grade and a total ride of 13 1/2 miles.

Advanced riders should consider a full loop starting with the six mile Toll Road Climb (see Ride 20). When Toll Road ends, just ride across Highway 341 onto Cartwright Road and follow it to Lousetown Road (as described above under "Trailhead"). The advanced rider's loop is as follows: (a) Toll Road Climb (6 miles); (b) Cartwright Road to the fire station (3 miles); (c) fire station to Mira Loma (8 3/4 miles); and (d) Mira Loma to Highway 341 and Toll Road (4 3/4 miles). This entire loop involves plenty of climbing and descending and a total of 22 3/4 miles.

Ride #23
LAGOMARSINO PETROGLYPHS

Difficulty: Advanced
Distance: 15 miles
Starting Elevation: 5790 feet
Highest Elevation: 6040 feet
Map: USGS Steamboat/Chalk Hills 7.5

Trailhead
Heading south from Reno on U.S. 395, drive 10 miles to the Mt. Rose Junction and turn left onto Highway 341 toward Virginia City. Climb Geiger Grade (341) up to the Virginia Highlands turnoff (about 7 miles) and turn left onto Cartwright Road. Follow Cartwright a little over 3 miles to its junction with Lousetown Road (fire station). There is plenty of parking near this intersection.

Difficulty
This ride is best suited to advanced mountain bikers. Although the entire run (out and back) is only 15 miles, very little of it is flat. With several ascents and descents, many of them very rocky, the highest elevation is 6040 feet and the lowest is 5040— there are repeated possibilities for novice riders to lose control and crash. Taken cautiously, with some walking

on steep hills, strong intermediates may also enjoy this ride.

Description
Deep in the Virginia Mountain Range which borders the Truckee Meadows (Reno-Sparks area) to the east is located one of the West's finest petroglyph sites. Petroglyphs ("rock writing") are figures, lines and symbols carved by Native Americans on the face of boulders. The designation "Lagomarsino" comes from the name of a rancher who in years past grazed cattle in the area. This site has hundreds of well-preserved petroglyphs dating between 2000 and 5000 years old. The canyon containing the rock art is believed to have been a game ambush site and the carvings are thought to represent magic to help the Indians in their hunt.

The ride begins at the fire station at the intersection of Cartwright Road and Lousetown Road. Go east on Cartwright, past Bull Frog to a road labeled Aurora (a little under one mile). Turn left onto Aurora and go to Panamint (1 1/4 miles from the fire station). Turn right and climb Panamint hill, then swing left at Bodie (just over 1 1/2 miles). Follow this road until you encounter a "T" (at about 4 miles), then turn right. Make sure you can find this turn again for your return trip. Stay on the main road, headed east, until you reach another "T" at six miles from the fire station. Turn left at this "T", then one-quarter mile later go left at the "Y". Ride north down toward the creek (you'll intersect and follow powerlines)— look for a blue wrecked car (at about 6 1/2 miles). This wreck

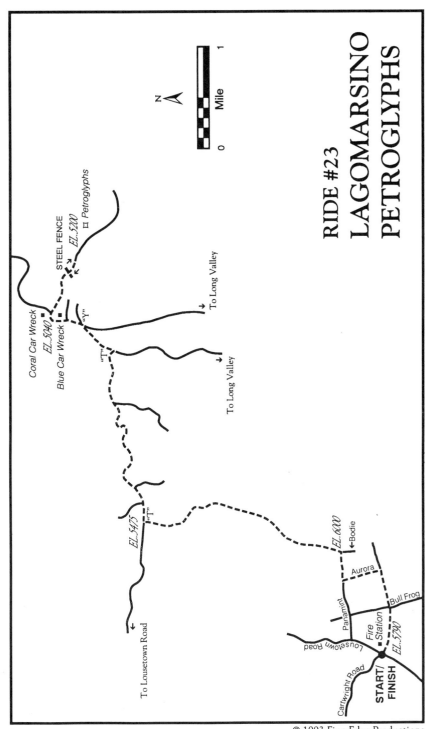

RIDE #23
LAGOMARSINO
PETROGLYPHS

N

0   Mile   1

☐ Petroglyphs

EL.5200

STEEL FENCE

Coral Car Wreck

EL.5040

Blue Car Wreck

"Y"

To Long Valley

"T"

To Long Valley

"T"

EL.5475

To Lousetown Road

EL.6000
←Bodie

Aurora

Panamint

Bull Frog

Fire
Station
EL.5790

Lousetown Road

Cartwright Road

START/
FINISH

marks an old homesite (consider a little exploring here to find some building remains, a beautiful tree-lined cottonwood canyon, and some remarkable hand-stacked rock fences).

Continue north past the blue wreck until you reach the coral colored car wreck (about one-quarter mile apart). The road swings right, past the coral wreck into a "Y"— take the road furthest to the right (immediately cross the creek bed then swing left, then right to start a slow steady climb up the canyon). On your left, at about 7 1/4 miles, you will see a small grouping of petroglyphs. Shortly thereafter you'll pass through a short steel fence and at just under 7 1/2 miles you will reach a large turnaround area. Take the road to the left (a short, steep down and up) and you will ride right alongside the main concentration of petroglyphs (7 1/2 miles). The carvings are almost non-stop from the road level all the way to the rimrock. Get off your bike, hike around and enjoy. You will see bighorn sheep, human figures, snakes, birds, circles, grids, rakes, spirals, lizards, groups of dots, and lots of lines both straight and wavy. For some, interpretations come easily; but for many of these carvings, you will have to stretch your imagination to figure out

Prehistoric rock art.

their mystical purpose. The area is a "designated archaelogical site", making vandalism here illegal as well as immoral. Please do not in any way alter or deface this remarkable prehistoric art museum— let's save it, in good condition, for the generations that follow us. If you witness any vandalism, please report it to the Storey County Sheriff's Office.

Ride #24
BARREL SPRINGS ROAD

Difficulty: Beginner
Distance: 8 miles
Starting Elevation: 6460 feet
Highest Elevation: 6460 feet
Map: USGS Virginia City/Flowery Peak 7.5

Trailhead
Heading south from Reno on U.S. 395, drive 10 miles to the Mt. Rose junction and turn left onto Highway 341 toward Virginia City. Climb Geiger Grade (341) and watch for the turnoff just short of two miles past the summit (Geiger Summit is identified by a highway sign). The turn is labeled "Lousetown Road"— make a left and park your vehicle in the parking area just off the highway.

Difficulty
This ride is suited to cyclists of all skill levels. It is fairly short (8 miles), requires minimal technical skills, and has just enough ascending and descending to make it interesting (high and low elevations vary only by 450 feet).

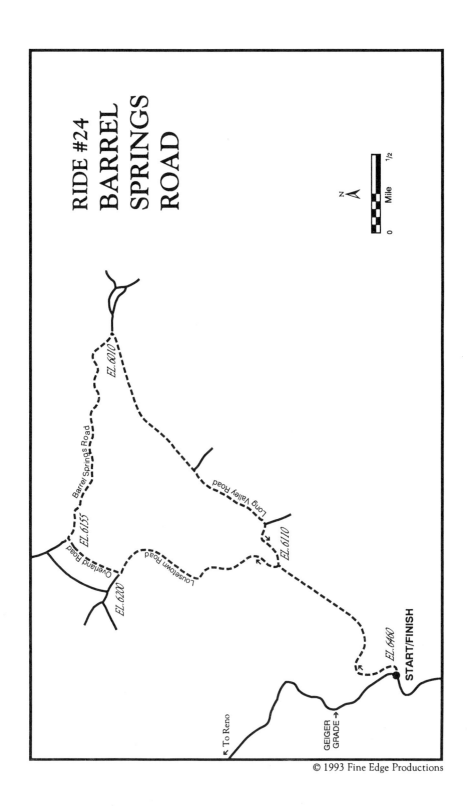

RIDE #24
BARREL
SPRINGS
ROAD

N

0   Mile   ½

Barrel Springs Road

EL. 6010

EL. 6155

Long Valley Road

Overland Road

EL. 6200

Lousetown Road

EL. 6110

EL. 6460

START/FINISH

To Reno

GEIGER GRADE →

© 1993 Fine Edge Productions

Novice cyclists should be careful going downhill; at slow speeds, this is a very safe ride.

Description

From Geiger Grade, head north on Lousetown Road (this is actually both Lousetown Road and Long Valley Road at this point). Go past River View Road (someone with a great sense of humor named this little side road). At a little over 1 1/4 miles you will encounter a fork—go left onto Lousetown Road to begin the "loop" part of this ride (the fork to the right is Long Valley Road). Wind gently uphill to the north. Check out the high desert pines and junipers and the interesting rock formations. Also, this area is famous for mustangs—there are wild horses to be seen here almost all year around!

Follow the wide, gravelled main road until it crests the top, giving a view of the Virginia Highlands (housing development). Shortly thereafter, at a little over 2 1/2 miles from the beginning of this ride, turn right onto Overland Road (just before Lousetown Road turns to pavement). At three miles you will encounter a "T"; turn right onto Barrel Springs Road. Very soon thereafter you will begin the descent into Long Valley. You will pass a brightly painted red rock (on your left) around 3 1/2 miles. At 4 1/2 miles Barrel Springs Road ends as it meets Long Valley Road. Turn right here and head southwest, back to the Lousetown Road/Long Valley Road fork. At just over 6 1/2 miles (at the above-mentioned fork) bear left. When you reach your starting point, the parking area next to Geiger Grade, you will have completed an eight mile ride.

Ride #25 LONG VALLEY LOOP

Difficulty: Advanced
Distance: 19 3/4 miles
Starting Elevation: 6460 feet
Highest Elevation: 6460 feet
Map: USGS Virginia City/Flowery Peak 7.5

Trailhead

Heading south from Reno on U.S. 395, drive 10 miles to the Mt. Rose junction and turn left onto Highway 341 toward Virginia City. Go up Geiger Grade

High desert oasis.

(341) and watch for the turn about two miles past the summit (Geiger Summit is identified by a highway sign). The turn is labeled "Lousetown Road"— make a left turn and park your vehicle in the parking area just off the highway.

Difficulty

This ride is best suited to cyclists with advanced technical skills and endurance. Less experienced riders frequently run the first few miles of it; the ride out to the rock corral and back is relatively flat and only 9 1/2 miles total distance. There are several sections beyond the rock corral that are steep uphill or downhill and/or very rocky— to avoid a lot of walking, you should have good technical riding ability and enough endurance to keep rolling for 20 miles. The highest elevation is at the start next to Geiger Grade (6460) and the lowest you will encounter is just prior to the halfway point, over 1300 feet less (5120 feet).

Description

For an enjoyable tour through the high desert this is a great ride. There are pines and junipers, fascinating rock formations, bubbling springs and green meadows, interesting little canyons, and so on. Virtually any time of the year you will see herds of wild horses— hundreds of mustangs live in this area. Begin your ride by heading north on Lousetown Road. When you encounter a fork at 1 1/4 miles, bear right onto Long Valley Road. Stay on this road as it heads northeast. You will pass under power lines at just over 3 3/4 miles. At about four miles begin a brief descent to the fork in the road around 4 1/2 miles. Go left at this "Y" and one fourth

of a mile later you will pass an "oasis"— look for the remains of a handbuilt rock corral and numerous trees just below it. Either now or on your return trip, consider some exploring. In the little canyon right behind the corral are natural year-around springs, tall trees, green grass, a little creek and a tiny pond.

From the rock corral take the road going northeast (alongside the power poles). Follow the powerlines and at almost 5 1/2 miles you'll pass the remains of an old wooden corral on your left; then at 5 3/4 miles you will encounter "Chalk Hills" on your right (very light colored low hills). There is a fork just before you pass these hills— the two roads rejoin (at 6 miles) so take either option here. At just under 6 1/4 miles, the road forks again (take the road to the left). The loop portion of this ride begins at 7 1/4 miles— as you're climbing bear right. Very soon thereafter you will crest the hill and then descend for several minutes. This downhill ends at 7 3/4 miles (you will go through a wash and immediately head uphill). You'll crest the next hill at 8 1/4 miles and encounter panoramic views to the north. The next mile and one-half is all downhill, sometimes steep and sometimes rocky.

At 9 3/4 miles from the start of this ride, next to a power pole structure with three poles, swing left under the powerlines (continuing straight ahead will take you to the Lagomarsino Petroglyphs). Do not turn right a few hundred feet later, but swing left and up a gentle hill. You will pass a right turn (it goes west to Lousetown Road)

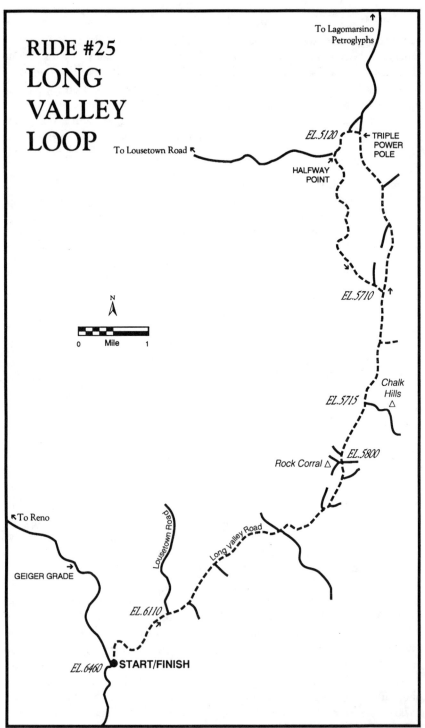

RIDE #25
LONG
VALLEY
LOOP

To Lagomarsino
Petroglyphs

To Lousetown Road

EL.5120

TRIPLE
POWER
POLE

HALFWAY
POINT

N

0   Mile   1

EL.5710

Chalk
Hills △

EL.5715

EL.5800

Rock Corral △

To Reno

Lousetown Road

Long Valley Road

GEIGER GRADE

EL.6110

EL.6460   START/FINISH

© 1993 Fine Edge Productions

at 10 miles— don't turn here, but note that this spot marks the halfway point on this ride.

Continue south and soon you will start a long two-mile uphill. Climb to the top, then descend briefly to reach the fork where the "loop" started. Go right to retrace your route all the way back to Geiger Grade. At about 14 miles you will pass the Chalk Hills again, and around 15 miles is the rock corral. When you reach 18 1/2 miles, Long Valley Road rejoins Lousetown Road and at just over 19 3/4 miles you will be back to where you started next to Geiger Grade.

House remains at Washington.

Ride #26
LOCKWOOD TO WASHINGTON

Difficulty: Intermediate
Distance: 9 miles
Starting Elevation: 4400 feet
Highest Elevation: 5070 feet
Map: USGS Vista/Steamboat/Chalk
      Hills 7.5

Trailhead
From Virginia Street, a few blocks north of the downtown Reno casinos, pick up I-80 headed east. Go past Sparks and into the foothills. Leave the freeway at the Lockwood Exit and go south across the Truckee River. Park along the right side of the road just after the bridge.

Difficulty
The second half of the 4 1/2 mile ride from Lockwood to the old mining camp of Washington requires basic technical skills to comfortably negotiate an old jeep road. In addition, cyclists will encounter some brief but steep climbing (450 feet in the last mile). Lockwood to Washington (and back) is suited to intermediates and better.

Description
This ride begins on pavement, in the small community of Lockwood, and ends on dirt at the remains of a tiny mining town in the Virginia Range. The Washington settlement was active during the late 1800's and was served by the post office in Virginia City. From Lockwood, ride south (then southwest) on the main paved road. At one-half mile you will cross a cattle guard— continue ahead on the paved road. At just over two miles there is a road going left (to the dump); you continue straight ahead onto gravel.

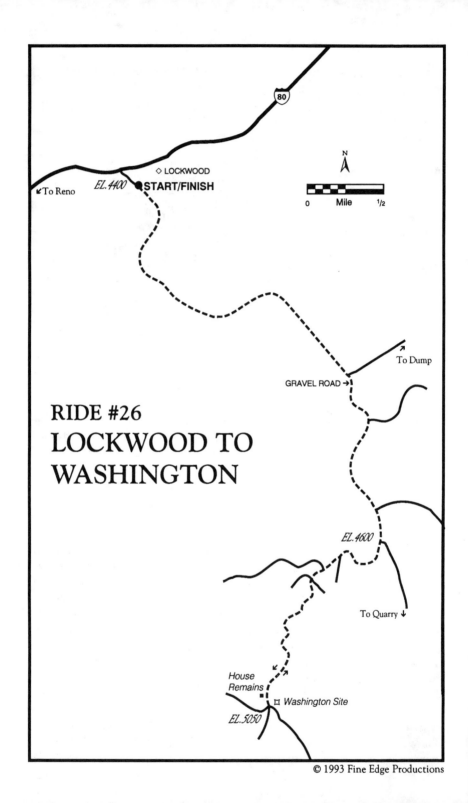

80

◇ LOCKWOOD
EL.4400 ●START/FINISH

To Reno

N

0   Mile   1/2

To Dump

GRAVEL ROAD →

RIDE #26
LOCKWOOD TO
WASHINGTON

EL.4600

To Quarry ↓

House
Remains

Washington Site

EL.5050

© 1993 Fine Edge Productions

Stay on the main road which swings to the right at 2 1/2 miles. You will cross a wash (usually dry) just over three miles from Lockwood— very shortly thereafter bear right onto a smaller road (if you miss this turn you will ride through large steel gates and up to a giant aggregate quarry). After bearing right the road leads up a picturesque little canyon dotted with desert pines and cedars and alongside a little creek.

At 3 1/2 miles ride through the creek (or dry wash) and shortly thereafter look to the left to see the foundation of a large old building. Around four miles from Lockwood you will ride through a small mining pit and then straight ahead, climbing up the left canyon wall. At about 4 1/2 miles is the old mining camp called Washington. The only significant remains are some hand-fitted building logs and a beautifully crafted rock fireplace and chimney. The area directly ahead and to your right is Washington. This ride stops here, an historic and scenic spot to take a break and explore a little before turning around and retracing your route back to Lockwood (a total ride of nine miles). If you would like more distance on this ride you can take off on any of a number of roads that head uphill out of the Washington site. For the adventurous, you can follow the roads that go south and intersect Lousetown Road near the Virginia Highlands, or go a couple of miles south then work west all the way to the Truckee Meadows (near Hidden Valley).

Ride #27
PANORAMA
POINT

Difficulty: Advanced
Distance: 8 miles
Starting Elevation: 4400 feet
Highest Elevation: 5100 feet
Map: USGS Vista/Steamboat 7.5

Trailhead

Take Virginia Street a few blocks north of downtown Reno and pick up I-80 headed east. Go past Sparks and into the foothills. Leave the freeway at the Lockwood Exit and go south (crossing the Truckee River). Park along the right side of the road just past the bridge over the river.

Difficulty

This ride is relatively short (8 miles), but requires some moderately difficult climbing and descending on rocky roads. Sections of these old jeep trails suffer considerable erosion and it does not appear that anyone is maintaining them. Thus, the ride to Panorama Point is suited to advanced riders or better. The route is essentially "out and back"— four miles of climbing (700 feet elevation gain) followed by four miles of descending— with one of the most dramatic views you'll ever see of the Truckee Meadows in between!

Description

The destination for this ride is a dead-end road in the Virginia Range. Beginning on pavement at the little town of Lockwood, you will ride up into the hills to a dramatic viewpoint at the

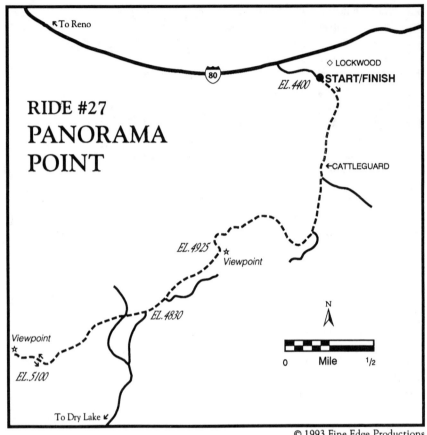

RIDE #27
PANORAMA POINT

© 1993 Fine Edge Productions

head of a canyon above Hidden Valley. From your starting point, ride south (toward the dump) on the main paved road. At about one-half mile the road has a cattleguard— cross it and continue ahead for a few hundred yards, then turn right onto a dirt road and begin climbing.

At 1 3/4 miles from Lockwood (after over 500 feet of elevation gain from the paved road), the road widens as you crest the hill. This is a "viewpoint" in that there are long-distance views to the north and east. After a short descent (just under a half mile), cross the

culverted wash and begin climbing again.

At just over 2 1/2 miles the road forks. To get to Panorama Point turn right at this fork (turning to the left takes you to a dry lake, the destination for Ride 28). Stay on the main road, ignoring smaller side roads. You will approach powerlines in this final part of your ascent and actually cross under them at about 3 1/2 miles from Lockwood. Continue climbing until the road dead ends into a mound of dirt straight ahead of you. Walk up onto the mound (or around it) and you will encounter a view of the Truckee Meadows dramatically framed by rock canyon walls. This is a great place to pause for refreshment and hydration.

The return route follows exactly the same one that brought you to Panorama Point. You can now practice your descending skills, for most of the return trip to Lockwood is downhill.

On your way back you'll will pass the fork at 5 3/4 miles and climb back up to the first viewpoint at a little over 6 1/4 miles. You will reach the pavement at 7 1/2 miles. When you finish the trip at Lockwood, you will have pedaled for a total ride of 8 miles.

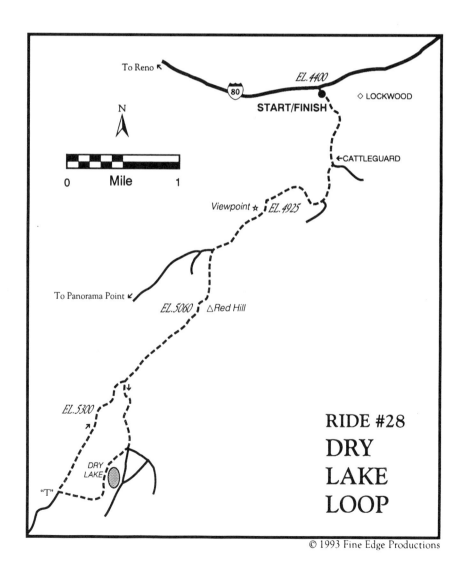

RIDE #28
DRY
LAKE
LOOP

Ride #28
DRY LAKE LOOP

Difficulty: Advanced
Distance: 10 1/2 miles
Starting Elevation: 4400 feet
Highest Elevation: 5300 feet
Map: USGS Vista/Steamboat 7.5

Trailhead
A few blocks north of downtown Reno, pick up I-80 headed east. Go past Sparks and into the foothills. Exit the freeway at Lockwood and go south, across the Truckee River. Park along the right side of the road just past the bridge over the river.

Difficulty
This ride into the Virginia Range to an unnamed highland dry lake and back is only 10 1/2 miles if you do not take any side trips. However, there are several moderately long uphill sections (total elevation gain of 900 feet) and some steep rocky downhills— it is well suited to cyclists with advanced technical riding skills or better. To increase the length of the ride, there are numerous side roads available for exploration.

Description
Summarizing this ride's route, the first one-third takes you to the area of the dry lake, the second one-third is a loop in that area, and the last one-third retraces the course you followed to get to the loop. From your starting point at Lockwood, next to the Truckee River, ride south toward the dump on the main paved road. At about one-half mile the road has a cattle guard— cross it and continue ahead for a few hundred yards, then turn right onto a dirt road and begin climbing. You will gain over 500 feet of elevation in the next mile and one-half. When you crest the hill, the wide spot in the road is a "viewpoint" looking to the north and to the east. After a short descent, cross the culverted wash and begin climbing again. At just over 2 1/2 miles the road forks. To get to the dry lake, turn left at this fork (a right turn takes you to Panorama Point, Ride 27).

Continue ahead on the main road, ignoring side roads going to the power poles. At just over 2 3/4 miles you will cross under the "major" powerlines (metal poles), about 100 yards later cross under "minor" powerlines (wooden poles), and about 100 yards later crest "Red Hill" (you will get a better look at its dramatic coloration on your return trip). You've reached the highlands and some of the next 1 1/4 mile is actually flat (as will be the area around the dry lake)! Keep a lookout through here, because herds of wild horses are frequently seen all through the highlands of the Virginia Range.

At just over 3 3/4 miles, bear left at the fork (don't turn right, up to the power poles)— it is here that you begin the "loop" part of this ride. Go up and over the little hill and you can see the dry lake. At 4 1/2 miles turn right and skirt along the right side of the dry lake bed. There is a four-way intersection of dirt roads at five miles from your starting point in Lockwood; to continue Dry Lake Loop turn right toward the powerlines. From this vantage point you can see other roads in the area— to lengthen your ride check some of them out. At just under 5 1/2 miles (just before the powerlines) you will encounter a "T". A left turn here will open up another area of numerous jeep trails for exploration and a route back to the Truckee Meadows (it comes out on Mira Loma between Hidden Valley and Virginia Foothills).

To continue Dry Lake Loop, turn right at the "T" and climb uphill gently, alongside the powerlines. The highest elevation reached in this ride (5300 feet) is achieved when you cross under the minor powerlines and start downhill. The next one-quarter mile is a brief but exciting descent back to the flat— at 6 1/2 miles the "loop" part of this ride ends and you will encounter the road that you followed earlier (turn left and head for Red Hill). Continuing toward Lockwood, you will be back at the fork to Panorama Point at 8 1/4 miles. Turn right and you'll be back on the pavement at 10 miles. Turn left, go across the cattle guard, and this ride ends at 10 1/2 miles where it started next to the Truckee River in Lockwood.

Ride #29
SIXMILE
CANYON

Difficulty: Advanced
Distance: 16 1/4 miles
Starting Elevation: 4340 feet
Highest Elevation: 6050 feet
Map: USGS Flowery Peak/Virginia City 7.5

Trailhead
There are numerous ways to approach this ride. Most popular are (a) an out and back from Virginia City to U.S 50,

Ghost town exploration.

Dry Lake in the Virginia Range.

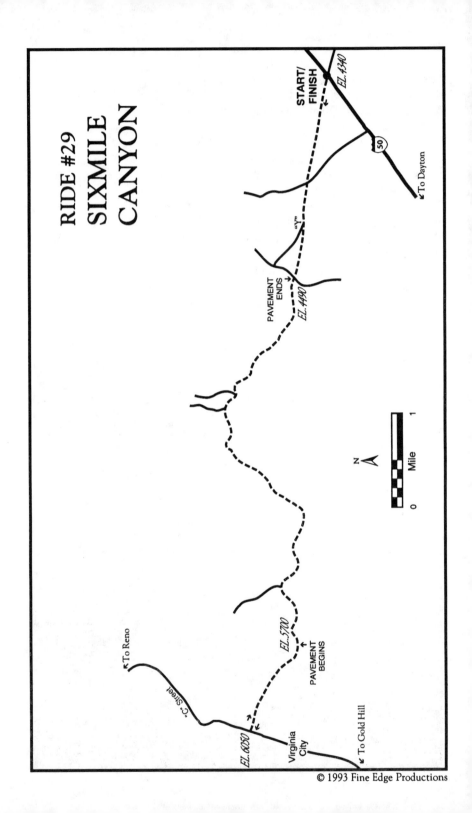

RIDE #29
SIXMILE
CANYON

START/
FINISH

EL. 4340

50

To Dayton

"Y"

PAVEMENT
ENDS
EL. 4490

N

0 Mile 1

To Reno

"C" Street

EL. 6050

Virginia
City

EL. 5700

PAVEMENT
BEGINS

To Gold Hill

© 1993 Fine Edge Productions

(b) for Reno/Sparks residents, being dropped at U.S. 50 and riding up to Virginia City, then taking Geiger Grade or Old Toll Road to get back home, or (c) parking your vehicle along U.S. 50 and riding up to Virginia City and back. The description that follows is based on the last routing. From U.S. 395 in Carson City, go east on U.S. 50. Six miles after going through Dayton, watch for signs indicating Sixmile Canyon. Turn left onto Sixmile Canyon Road and park your vehicle.

Difficulty
This ride is suited to advanced or better riders. Although it is not technically demanding, it is of sufficient distance and the climb (1710 feet) is such that strength and conditioning are important.

Description
Although this ride begins and ends on pavement in housing areas, a large portion of it is on dirt through a delightful high desert canyon complete with trees, shrubs, and other flora, and a year-around babbling brook. Sixmile Canyon was named for its length (during Virginia City's heyday, about 1850). The Comstock Lode was discovered in Ophir Ravine near the head of the

canyon and its road linked the entire mining area with Eagle Valley and the Carson River below.

This ride begins at Sixmile Canyon Road's intersection with U.S. 50. Head west on the paved road. At 1 3/4 miles you will encounter a "Y"—go left (right is Rowan Gulch). At two miles and after 150 feet of elevation gain, the pavement ends. Continue up the canyon, staying on the main road, following the creek. Enjoy a beautiful and scenic desert canyon for the next several miles!

At just under 7 1/2 miles, the pavement resumes (you have completed 1360 feet of climbing). Continue ahead, uphill, past "L" street, past "D" street. At just over 8 miles you will reach "C" street (Highway 341, Virginia City's main street). At this point you will have gained over 1700 feet in elevation from your starting point. If you turn around here and head back down Sixmile Canyon to U.S. 50 you will finish an out and back ride of 16 1/4 miles. If you have the time, consider a bicycle tour of Virginia City, a fascinating old mining town. It's a delightful pause before your long descent back to the ride's starting point.

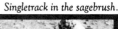

Singletrack in the sagebrush.

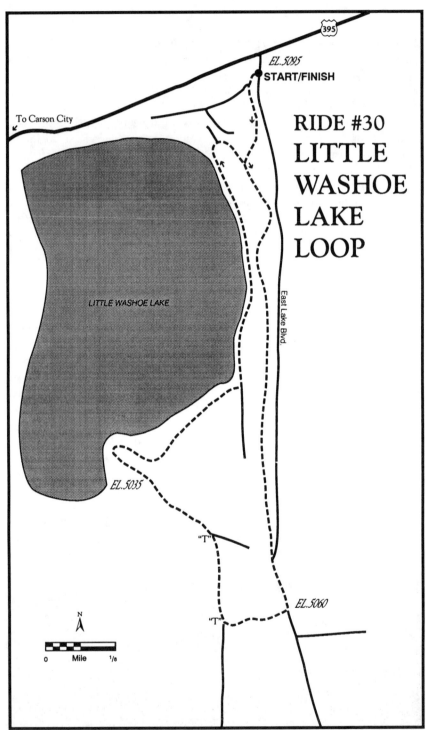

395

EL.5095
START/FINISH

To Carson City

RIDE #30
LITTLE
WASHOE
LAKE
LOOP

East Lake Blvd.

LITTLE WASHOE LAKE

EL.5035

"T"

EL.5060

"T"

N

0   Mile   1/8

© 1993 Fine Edge Productions

5 WASHOE COUNTY

CHAPTER

Ride # 30 Little Washoe Lake Loop; # 31 Washoe Lake Foothills; #32 Jumbo Grade Climb.

Heading south about 20 miles from downtown Reno on Highway 395, you crest a hill and descend to Washoe Valley where you have an expansive view of Little Washoe Lake, Washoe Lake and the Virginia Range to the east. To the west of the highway, green pastures and meadows meet the base of the Carson Range. There is very little riding available to the west. However, east of 395, numerous old mining roads and jeep trails provide access to the historic Virginia Range. Routes leading around the two Washoe Lakes and up Jumbo Grade (the most popular route leading from the valley to the high country) offer enjoyment and challenges for all levels of ability.

Ride #30 LITTLE WASHOE LAKE LOOP

Difficulty: Beginner
Distance: 2 1/4 miles
Starting Elevation: 5095 feet
Highest Elevation: 5095 feet
Map: USGS Washoe City 7.5

Trailhead
Little Washoe Lake is located at the north end of Washoe Lake, just off of U.S. 395 about 20 minutes south of Reno. To get to the lake, drive south from Reno, to a point 6 1/2 miles south of the intersection of 395 and Mt. Rose Highway (431). Turn left onto East Lake Boulevard, go about 50 yards (just past the cattleguard) and turn right and park.

Difficulty
This is an easy ride, suited to cyclists of all ability levels. The route is nearly

Little Washoe Lake.

Portage through the creek.

flat (60 feet elevation change) and the dirt roads relatively smooth. The total length of the loop is just over 2 1/4 miles— consider adding some exploring on other roads or multiple loops to increase the workout.

Description

Little Washoe Lake Loop is both scenic and interesting, and is directly north of the Scripps Wildlife Management Area. To begin, from East Lake go toward Little Washoe Lake by bearing left at the fork (to the right is a narrow paved road, an option if you would like to explore the north end of the lake). Bearing left directs you south— at one-quarter mile don't turn right, keep going south (parallel to East Lake). At just over three-fourths of a mile you will briefly join East Lake Boulevard. Ride along the shoulder for a few

hundred feet, watching for the first right turn. Go right across the cattleguard (past the Scripps sign), then stay as far left as possible. Ride west following the powerlines.

At one mile is a "T"— turn right to continue your loop (a left turn takes you on a side trip into the Scripps State Wildlife Management Area). About 500 feet past your right turn, go straight at the 4-way intersection of little, two-rut jeep roads. After another 500 feet go straight ahead at the 5-way intersection, followed a few yards later by a left at the "T". You will now be heading northwest, toward the nearby southern tip of Little Washoe Lake (toward the housing development in the distance). At 1 1/3 mile, when you reach the big open area at the edge of the lake, turn right and head north along the lake. Stay right alongside the lake until a little over 1 1/2 miles—here the road swings right then resumes paralleling the lake (but not along the edge at first). Continue north and the route will resume coursing along the edge of the lake. At just over 2 miles the road turns to deep sand and ends at a "T"—turn right and go up the hill. At just under 2 1/4 miles you will intersect the main road you started on. Turn left and you will be back at the start (having ridden a total of 2 1/4 miles plus any sidetrips).

Ride #31
WASHOE LAKE FOOTHILLS

Difficulty: Intermediate
Distance: 3 miles
Starting Elevation: 5080 feet
Highest Elevation: 5540 feet
Map: USGS Washoe City 7.5

Trailhead

To reach the starting point for this ride, go south on U.S. 395 from Reno

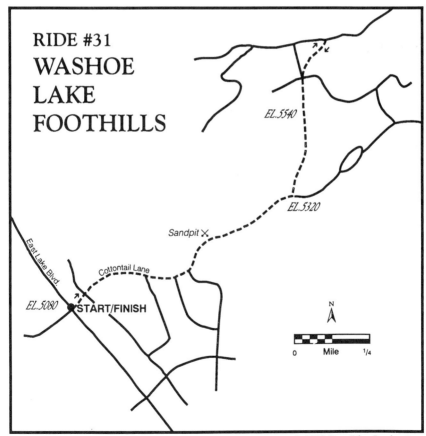

RIDE #31
WASHOE LAKE FOOTHILLS

EL.5540
EL.5320
Sandpit X
East Lake Blvd
Cottontail Lane
EL.5080 START/FINISH

N

0   Mile   1/4

to East Lake Boulevard (a left turn off of 395, about 15 miles south of downtown Reno). Take East Lake south, past Little Washoe Lake, about 2 1/2 miles, to Cottontail Lane. Turn left (east) onto Cottontail and park along the side of the road. An alternative starting point if you want to avoid riding on pavement is to park on Cottontail where the blacktop ends.

Difficulty

This ride has an elevation gain of nearly 500 feet and is suited to intermediates or better. It is a relatively short out and back (3 miles total) with numerous trails (both single and double-track) for side trips, hill climbing, finding alternate routes back to the start, and so on. Dozens of roads and trails exist out here, primarily because of extremely heavy motorcycle activity.

Description

This is a very popular mountain biking and motorcycle dirt biking area for Washoe Lake residents. From this area's high points there are great views of the entire Washoe Valley with Slide Mountain and Mt. Rose as the backdrop. From the intersection of East Lake and Cottontail, go northeast on Cottontail, past Brenda, Chukar, Buckskin, and Chipmunk streets. At just under one-half mile the road turns to dirt. At one-half mile you will ride past a sandpit (on your left)—continue uphill on the main road.

At just under one mile you bear left at the fork and go north. At 1 1/4 miles go straight at the 4-way intersection, and a few feet later go right at the fork. The end of this out and back ride is the

bottom of the hill, a distance of 1 1/2 mile from East Lake. From this turn-around point you may wish to go east to explore or north for some extremely tough hill climbing. It is possible to find an alternate route back to East Lake, beginning by heading left down the canyon. With some difficulty you can work your way west and south to a powerline road which connects to a housing development. Once you reach the houses continue west until you encounter Brenda Way—go south on it all the way to Cottontail.

Ride #32
JUMBO GRADE CLIMB

Difficulty: Advanced
Distance: 6 1/2 miles
Starting Elevation: 5160 feet
Highest Elevation: 6120 feet
Map: USGS Washoe City/Virginia City 7.5

Trailhead

To reach the starting point for this ride, go south on U.S. 395 from Reno to East Lake Blvd. (a left turn off of 395, about 15 miles south of downtown Reno). Take East Lake south, about four miles, to Jumbo Grade (identified by a street sign). There is plenty of space across East Lake to park vehicles.

Difficulty

This ride is for advanced or better cyclists. It is only 6 1/2 miles long, but involves nearly 1000 feet of elevation gain in the first 3 1/2 miles and some steep downhilling on your return trip.

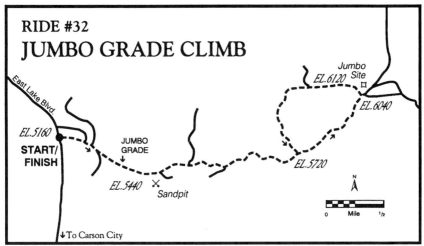

RIDE #32
JUMBO GRADE CLIMB

© 1993 Fine Edge Productions

Description

The Jumbo Grade Climb takes you into the Virginia Range to a loop through an area with numerous old mines. The flat along the creek below the mines was the location of an early twentieth-century camp named Jumbo. There was a post office there from April 1908 to November 1910. The nearby mines include Boss Jumbo, Mahoney, Campbell, Empire, and Pandora.

To begin this ride take the paved road east. At just under one-half mile bear left, across the cattleguard, onto a dirt road— stay on the main road, riding along the wash. You will reach another fork at one mile. Bear left to stay along the wash (don't turn right through an iron gate, into a sandpit). Through this area there are many side roads (made by motorcycles and 4-wheel drive vehicles) to play on if you choose, but your primary route continues on up the canyon, along the wash. Springs and trees and shrubs make this part of the ride very scenic. At two miles you will cross the wash— year-around, even in a drought, there is some spring water flowing here. Just ahead is a fork. Go right and through the wash again (continue on the main road, staying along the tree-lined wash/creek).

At just over 2 1/2 miles, just past large concrete pylons on your right, you will reach another fork. The left is a very steep, short hill (it goes up and out of the wash and is badly rutted)— you can bear right, avoiding the little hill, and ride in the wash, if there is not much water in it. After about 100 yards the road is up above the wash again; continue up the canyon. At three miles your trail goes sharp right, downhill through the wash and back up. Here you will enter a small, relatively flat area— ahead and to your left is the site of the mining camp called Jumbo. This is a great area to explore, in and around the Jumbo site. If you go right (east) and up the hill (about one and one-third mile) you will reach a spring (grassy area and pond); if you continue east it is possible to connect with Ophir Grade leading into Virginia City. If you go straight, you will encounter numerous trails and roads which ultimately can lead east toward Virginia City or west to Washoe Valley.

Immediately past the down and up through the wash at three miles is a left turn (goes northwest)— to continue your loop, turn onto that road and ride through the wash. Follow the main road winding up the hill and bear right at just over 3 1/4 miles (go left if you want to explore some of the work of the Pandora Mine). After bearing right at 3 1/4 miles you will bear left at another fork at 3 1/2 miles and ride past a dangerous, fenced mine shaft (it will be on your right). Just after you bear left, look ahead and you will see a road winding up the hill in front of you— that is your route (to the south; and you can see Slide Mountain and Mt. Rose on your right to the west). At the top of the hill stay on the main road swinging left, then right and down the hill to the south (as you descend you can see Jumbo Grade down below)— this is a serious, steep descent. You will encounter a

fork at just under four miles where you can go left, toward the concrete pylons to get back down to the bottom of the canyon. At four miles, turn right onto Jumbo Grade and head toward East Lake. At 5 3/4 miles you will pass the iron gate/sandpit again. At just over 6 1/4 miles you will ride over the cattleguard and back onto pavement. The ride ends when you rejoin East Lake Boulevard— if you did not explore or take any side trips, your ride was 6 1/2 miles long.

Below; Road to Jumbo. Above; Danger: Open mine shaft.

6 CARSON CITY

Ride #33 Virginia and Truckee Loop; #34 McClellan Peak Climb; #35 Carson River Loop; #36 Brunswick Canyon Climb; #37 Prison Hill River Run; #38 Clear Creek Road; #39 Kings Canyon Climb.

Carson City, Nevada's State Capital, sits in a valley surrounded by the Carson Range to the west and Pine Nut Range to the east. Similar to the Reno/Sparks area, rides to the west lead to mountains and pine forests and offer great summer riding. Although large tracts to the west formerly used by mountain bikers have been closed to public access over the past few years, the King's Canyon Climb remains open and is one of the truly great rides described in this guidebook. The area east of Carson City is still pretty much wide open, and you can find roads and jeep trails here that seem to go on forever. Among the most popular rides in this part of the State are those that follow the Carson River, including the Carson River Loop.

Ride #33 VIRGINIA AND TRUCKEE LOOP

Difficulty: Beginner
Distance: 3 3/4 miles
Starting Elevation: 4950 feet
Highest Elevation: 5100 feet
Map: USGS Carson City 7.5

Trailhead

This very popular ride is located at the northeast corner of Eagle Valley, about 28 miles south of Reno, on the outskirts of Carson City. From the Nevada State Capitol (domed building) in Carson City, take U.S. 395 (Carson Street) north for one mile to Winnie Lane and turn west. Turn right (north) onto Ormsby Boulevard. Go past Nye to swing left onto Combs Canyon Road—go a little over one-half mile to Murphy

Drive (sign is on the left) and turn right to park your vehicle.

Difficulty

This ride is suited to cyclists of all ability levels. It is neither long nor technically difficult, but offers an interesting desert ride with an assortment of "trails" (pavement, jeep road and single track are all represented).

Description

The driving economic force for Northern Nevada in the last century was the mining industry in and around Virginia City. In January of 1870 the Virginia and Truckee Railroad was operating between Gold Hill (a town adjacent to Virginia City) and Carson City. Two years later the line was run north to Reno which connected it to the much larger Central Pacific Railroad and thus to the whole nation. The first half of this mountain bike ride is on the

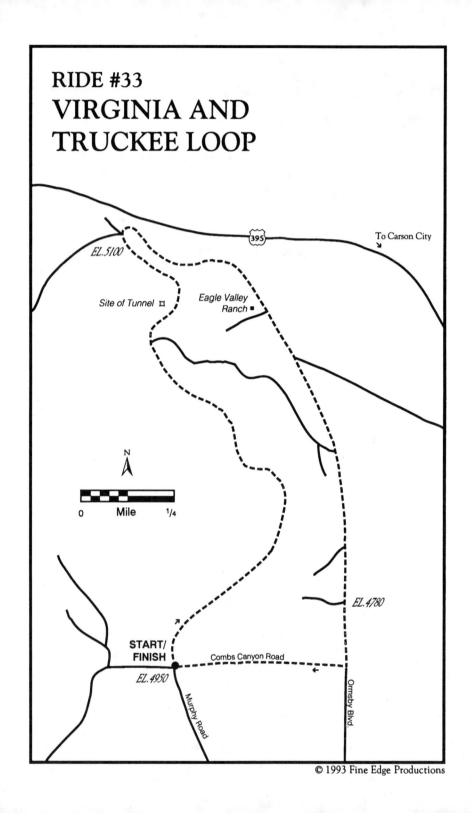

RIDE #33
VIRGINIA AND
TRUCKEE LOOP

To Carson City

EL. 5100

Site of Tunnel

Eagle Valley
Ranch

N

0   Mile   1/4

EL. 4780

START/
FINISH

Combs Canyon Road

EL. 4950

Murphy Road

Ormsby Blvd

© 1993 Fine Edge Productions

old "V & T" grade— occasionally cyclists and hikers still find railroad spikes here.

To begin your ride, go north onto the small dirt road, which shortly will head northeast. At one-half mile go right (uphill) onto singletrack. At 1 1/4 mile ignore the steep downhill to the right— a few hundred feet past here, on your left, there used to be a tunnel for the railroad (it was caved in by dynamite over a decade ago because it had become unsafe). At 1 1/2 miles is a fork. If you bear left, to continue on the old railroad grade, there is a dead-end just ahead. It is possible to go sharply left onto a singletrack just before the end, to go up and over the hill to connect with Combs Canyon Road. Or you can continue ahead at the end (go over the fence), and you will very shortly be in a housing development called Lakeview Estates. If you want the easiest possible ride, when you reach the dead end turn around and ride the same route back to the start (3 miles total, with no significant hills).

To continue the Virginia and Truckee Loop, turn right to go downhill at the fork you encountered at 1 1/2 miles (you will first go north, then U-turn to go south down the tree-lined canyon). At just over 1 3/4 miles you will pass a beige colored water storage tank. At just over 2 miles, this route takes you past the Eagle Valley Children's Home. There is a fork at 2 3/4 miles (left goes to U.S. 395)— bear right to keep going south. Stay on this road, passing by a green iron gate, until you reach Combs Canyon Road (stop sign) at just over 3 miles. Turn right and ride uphill, back

to where you began at Murphy Road. The entire loop, without side trips, is just under 3 3/4 miles long.

Ride #34
McCLELLAN
PEAK CLIMB

Difficulty: Advanced
Distance: 13 miles
Starting Elevation: 4880 feet
Highest Elevation: 7465 feet
Map: USGS New Empire/ Virginia City 7.5

Trailhead
McClellan Peak is a mountain about seven miles north (and slightly east) of downtown Carson City. From the center of town (Capitol Building), take U.S. 395 (Carson Street) north for 2 1/2 miles and turn east on Airport Road. Near the airport, turn left on Goni Road. Take Goni until the pavement ends (at Fermi Road). Park on the dirt road and begin your cycling here.

Difficulty
This ride is not technically difficult, but involves a lot of climbing. The route is out and back (more accurately, up and down), with each direction totaling 6 1/2 miles. However, the first 6 1/2 miles (the "out") involves an elevation gain of over 2500 feet. This ride is suited to advanced riders or better.

Description
As noted above, the McClellan Peak Climb is a long uphill (to the top of the

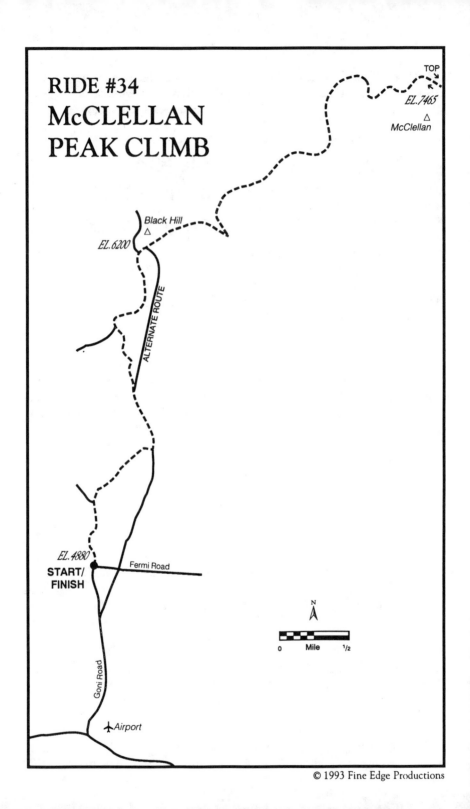

RIDE #34
McCLELLAN PEAK CLIMB

TOP

EL. 7465

△
McClellan

Black Hill
△

EL. 6200

ALTERNATE ROUTE

EL. 4880
START/ FINISH

Fermi Road

N

0 ——— Mile ——— ½

Goni Road

✈ Airport

View from McClellan Peak.

climbing and stay on the main road all the way to the top. At 6 miles you will find numerous electronic dishes and towers, on every high point around you. Continue on the main road, to the east, to get to the highest point. It is at the end of the road, a fenced electronic station with an elevation of 7465 (6 1/2 miles from where you started). There are numerous roads around the top if you are inclined to do some exploring. For the return trip, now that the climbing is over, consider taking in some of the dramatic panoramic views afforded by this ride. There are views in every direction— from varying vantage points, you should be able to see the Truckee Meadows (Reno area), Washoe Valley, Eagle Valley (Carson City area), the Carson Range (Mt. Rose, Slide Mountain, Genoa Peak), some of the Virginia City mining area, and so on.

The return to where you started is for the most part downhill. When you reach the U-turn just below Black Hill (10 1/4 miles from your starting point, 3 3/4 miles from the top of the mountain), remember the option for a brief (about one mile) alternate route along the creek— just drop into the canyon at the turn. The ride ends when you reach the pavement at the intersection of Goni and Fermi, for a total ride of 13 miles.

mountain), followed by a long downhill which retraces your route up. You start your climb by heading north on a gravel road (the continuation of Goni). After a few hundred yards you will pass a green water storage tank (on your left). At just under one-half mile you ride under powerlines and then come upon a fork— stay on the main road (bear right). At 1 3/4 miles there are roads to the right, going down to the creek (on your way back there is a short alternate route along that creek). The road U- turns to the right at Black Hill (at 2 3/4 miles— the alternate route mentioned above ends here). Stay on the main road headed uphill.

There are left turns that you should ignore at just under 3 miles, at 3 1/4 miles, and at 3 3/4 miles. Continue

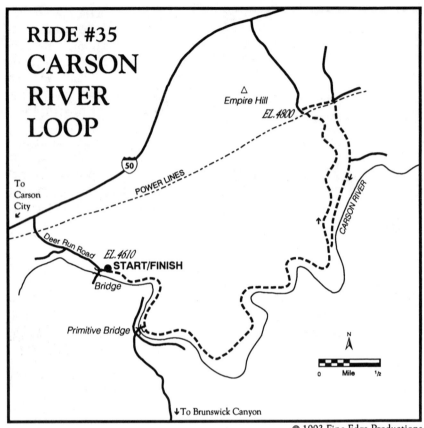

RIDE #35
CARSON
RIVER
LOOP

△ Empire Hill
EL.4800

50

To
Carson
City

POWER LINES

CARSON RIVER

Deer Run Road
EL.4610
START/FINISH

Bridge

Primitive Bridge

N

0   Mile   ¹/₂

↓ To Brunswick Canyon

© 1993 Fine Edge Productions

Ride #35
CARSON RIVER LOOP

Difficulty: Intermediate
Distance: 10 1/2 miles
Starting Elevation: 4610 feet
Highest Elevation: 4800 feet
Map: USGS New Empire 7.5

Trailhead

This ride is located a few miles east of Carson City, just off U.S. 50. To get to the starting point from U.S. 395 (Carson Street), go east on U.S. 50 (William Street). Go past Airport Road and 4 1/4 miles from 395 turn right (south) on Deer Run Road. You will encounter a bridge about three-quarters of a mile after the turn— park along the river, just before and to the left of the bridge.

Difficulty

The Carson River Loop is a medium length (10 1/2 miles) and only moderately difficult ride. It is suited to intermediate level cyclists or better.

Top; Ghost ranch along the Carson River.
Right; Carson River Canyon.

Description

If you appreciate desert rivers, you will
appreciate this ride. It provides interesting scenery from start to finish, and
there is always a possibility of catching
a glimpse of a wide assortment of wild
creatures (including rattlesnakes). This
ride begins by heading east from the
bridge, on a wide gravel road. At one
mile you will see a primitive bridge
going across the river. If you cross it and
follow the road up Brunswick Canyon,
you'll encounter a maze of jeep trails—
cyclists can explore for hours up there.
Also across the bridge, there are roads
going right alongside the river in both
directions for more exploration opportunities. To continue the Carson River
Loop, do not cross the bridge, but continue straight ahead (the road gets
smaller and rougher).

At 1 3/4 miles the road will swing away
from the river— to accomplish this, go
straight at the 4-way intersection (you
won't ride past a tunnel-looking structure ahead on the left, but turn away

from the river before it). At two miles
from your starting point you will pass a
large, abandoned concrete structure (on
your left). Go straight through here. A
few hundred yards later you will be
along the river again. Continue on the
main road. The road will soon begin to
climb steadily up the canyon wall, staying parallel with the Carson River. At
just over 3 3/4 miles the road swings

left, through a narrow draw. As you exit the draw you will see a road on your right—don't turn now, but note that it is the road that completes the loop part of this ride. Continue ahead, staying up high above the river.

At a little over 4 1/2 miles you will ride under low powerlines (right next to a power pole), then watch for a sharp right turn (headed downhill, following the powerlines). Drop down and go through the creek and back up to a 4-way intersection— turn right here and head down a little canyon, along (and sometimes through) the wash. You will exit the canyon at just over 5 1/2 miles and work your way down to the river's edge. Once you reach the river, you can turn left and ride east if you want to extend the ride and explore along the river. However, to continue the Carson River Loop, once you reach the river you are prevented from turning right— pause here for a rest break if you like, but then you must double back up the little canyon a few hundred feet to pick up a road headed westerly (up and over the hill, then down to the river's edge). Ride upstream (southwesterly) along the river.

At 6 1/4 miles you must turn right and start up the hill. If you miss this turn, the road along the river dead ends. There is a fork at 6 1/2 miles— go right and continue climbing back to the main road (left goes down to the river). Look to your left at just under 6 3/4 miles to see the rock foundation remains of an old, turn of the century ranch house. At just over 6 3/4 miles go right at the fork and keep climbing (left is another road down to the river's edge).

You will finish the loop portion of this ride, rejoining the main road at 7 miles. Turn left and go back through the narrow draw— from this point you will retrace your route all the way back to where the ride started. At 8 1/2 miles you will pass the large concrete structure again. At 9 1/2 miles you will ride by the bridge to Brunswick Canyon. One mile later you will reach your starting point, for a total ride of 10 1/2 miles.

RIDE #36 BRUNSWICK CANYON CLIMB

Difficulty: Advanced
Distance: 16 miles
Starting Elevation: 4610 feet
Highest Elevation: 6057 feet
Map: USGS New Empire/
    McTarnahan Hill 7.5

Trailhead
The starting point for this ride is a few miles east of Carson City. From U.S. 395 (Carson Street), go east on U.S. 50 (William Street). Go past Airport Road and 4 1/4 miles from 395 turn right on Deer Run Road. After just under three-quarters of a mile you will encounter a bridge across the Carson River. Do not cross the bridge— park your vehicle just to the left (downstream) of it.

Difficulty
The Brunswick Canyon Climb is best suited to advanced or better riders. It is not extremely long (out and back is 16 miles) and does not require high level technical skills, but involves over 1400

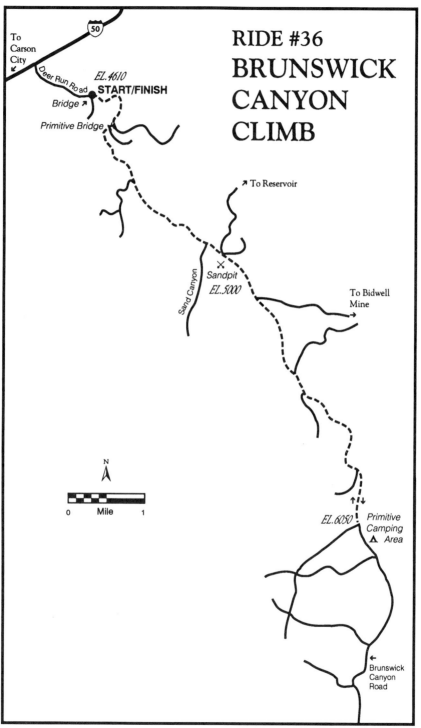

To Carson City

50

Deer Run Road

EL.4610
START/FINISH

Bridge ↗

Primitive Bridge

RIDE #36
BRUNSWICK CANYON CLIMB

↗ To Reservoir

Sand Canyon

✕
Sandpit
EL.5000

To Bidwell Mine →

N

0   Mile   1

EL.6050

Primitive Camping
△ Area

Brunswick Canyon Road

feet of elevation gain. If you add some of the side trips (described below) the ride is for expert cyclists only.

Description

Brunswick Canyon begins at the edge of Eagle Valley, along the Carson River and in sagebrush-covered hills, and ends up in a high desert forest. Portions of this ride provide the cyclist with beautiful panoramic views and interesting landscapes. In addition to the basic climb, two popular side trips (of several available) are also described.

From your parking area near the bridge, head east (downstream) on the wide dirt road along the river. At one mile, you will encounter another bridge (this one is narrow and primitive)— turn right and ride across the bridge. Immediately after crossing, go left. A few hundred feet after crossing the bridge continue straight ahead into Brunswick Canyon (don't turn left to stay along the river). From this point on, except for side trips, always follow the main road, along the wash/creek, steadily heading up the canyon.

At two miles you will see a sharp right turn (uphill). Do not turn; ride ahead and through the sandy wash and continue up the canyon. Ignore the road to the right at just over three miles (it goes into Sand Canyon, and can be followed south then west back to the Carson River). Continue straight ahead, up Brunswick Canyon Road. You will reach a large sandpit at 3 1/4 miles. To continue the Brunswick Canyon Climb go straight ahead, staying near the base of the canyon.

At the sandpit, there are two roads leading uphill (a sharp left and a gentle left). If you want an interesting side trip take either (they merge uphill). If you take the sharp left turn for a steep climb, and then stay on the main road after they merge, you will reach a pole gate after three-quarters of a mile. Continue ahead, and around the corner is a beautiful reservoir. This side trip (out and back) adds about 2 1/2 miles to your ride (and another 175 feet of elevation gain).

Continuing up Brunswick Canyon from the sandpit (the 3 1/4 mile mark), you will pass a rock quarry (on your left) at just under 3 3/4 miles. At just under four miles is another side trip option— the road headed uphill to the left goes to the Bidwell Mine. It is only 1 3/4 miles to the large flat above the mining area, but it involves an elevation gain of over 450 feet! If you take this side trip (out and back), you've added 3 1/2 miles to your ride total.

Over the next few miles there are other side trip options, if you wish to do more exploring, but consider holding off until you reach the flat at the road's crest (there's lots of room to roam up there). Continuing up Brunswick Canyon, the road will narrow and deteriorate. Your goal is the road's highest point, up in a forest of pines and cedars. Once you crest (at almost exactly eight miles), not only does the road no longer climb but you will see a giant large flat (mostly to the right of the road). Checking mileage to this point is important because there is a smaller flat (a false summit) a little ways before you reach the much larger flat which is the turnaround point for this ride. Once you reach the crest (at about 6050 feet elevation), just ahead on the left is a camping area in the trees (identified by a bright yellow wrecked vehicle)— a great place to pause and refresh before you begin your downhill run. As noted earlier there are side trip options available up in the high country. There is a road skirting the other side of the flat, running parallel with the road that you have been riding on, and four crossing roads which access it. These roads make possible a variety of exploration loops.

After reaching the crest of the Brunswick Canyon Road, the remainder of the ride is a long downhill run! Riders without strong descending skills should avoid high speeds through rocky or sandy sections of road. You will pass the Bidwell Mine road at 12 miles and the sandpit at 12 3/4 miles. When you cross the bridge over the Carson River, you will have ridden 15 miles (excluding any side trips). The end of the ride, at Deer Run Road, finishes an eight-mile return trip from the top of the canyon (for a total mileage of 16).

Ride #37
PRISON HILL
RIVER RUN

Difficulty: Beginner
Distance: 5 1/4 miles
Starting Elevation: 4600 feet
Highest Elevation: 4675 feet
Map: USGS New Empire/
    McTarnahan Hill 7.5

Trailhead

From downtown Carson City (one-fourth of a mile south of Nevada State Capitol on U.S. 395) take 5th Street east for 2 1/2 miles. You will pass the prison and pass Edmonds Street, then turn right onto Carson River Road. Go 2 1/2 miles (to the east side of Prison Hill), then turn right just after crossing the river. Drive down and park near the water.

Difficulty

This ride is very scenic, and not very difficult. The total elevation gain is less than 80 feet for the entire route and the full distance (out and back combined) is 5 1/4 miles. However, there are dozens of side roads for those desiring a longer ride. The Prison Hill River Run is suited to cyclists of all experience and skill levels.

Description

Desert rivers have a charm all of their own. Along the banks you will find numerous trees and shrubs that do not grow up the sagebrush-covered hillsides. Also, the presence of a waterway in arid country will usually provide an opportunity to view all sorts of wildlife— from rattlesnakes to coyotes to golden eagles. Starting at the parking area next to the bridge, head south on the dirt road along the river. At one-quarter mile you will ride under the powerlines— stay on the main road, following those powerlines. The giant hill along the other side of the river is Prison Hill. At just over 1 1/4 miles you will go under the powerlines again and be right along the river. At just over 1 1/2 miles you will encounter roads to the right. These go down to

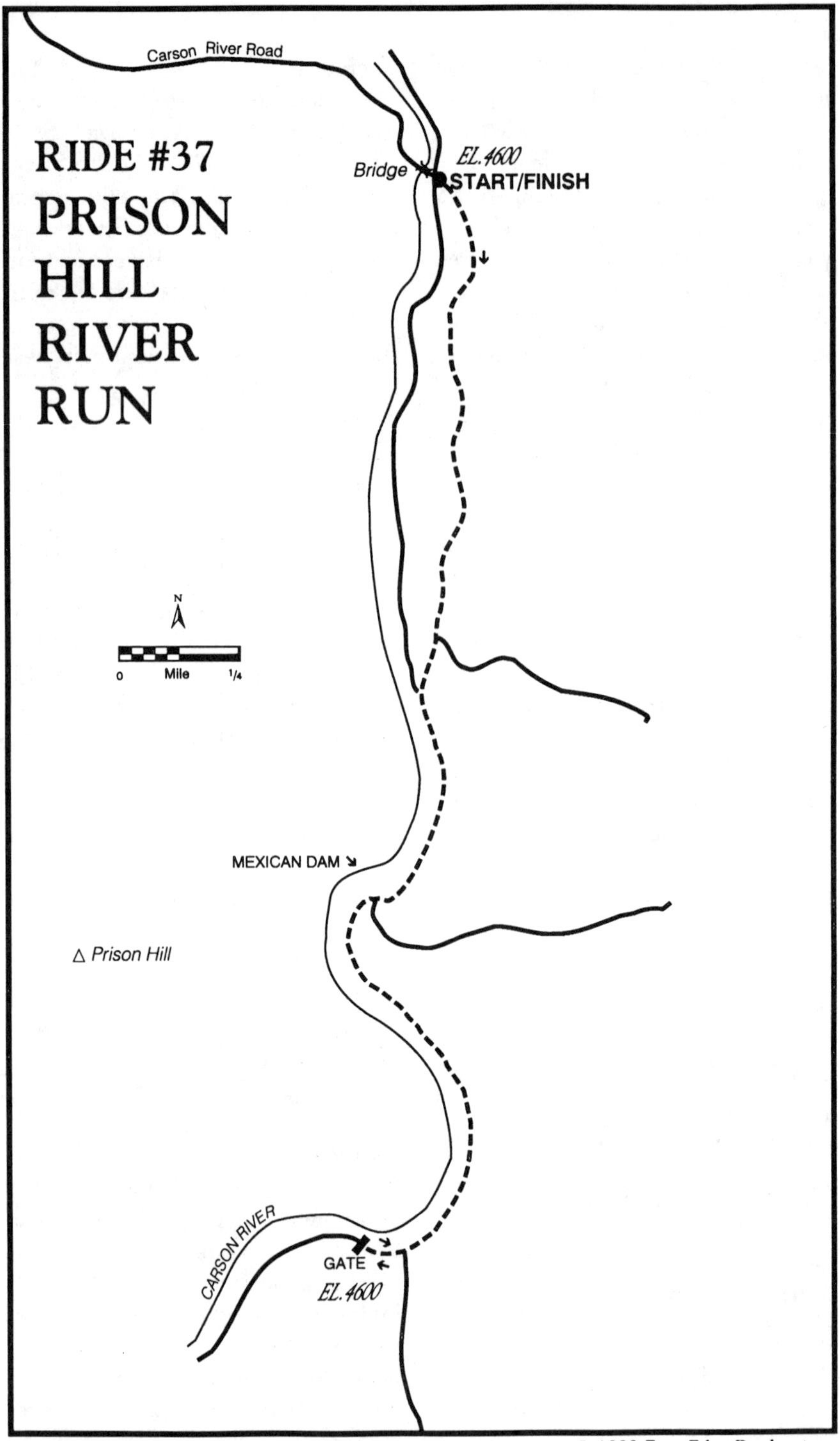

Carson River Road
RIDE #37
PRISON
HILL
RIVER
RUN
Bridge
EL. 4600
START/FINISH
N
0
Mile
1/4
MEXICAN DAM
Prison Hill
CARSON RIVER
GATE
EL. 4600

© 1993 Fine Edge Productions

Sunset at Mexican Dam.

"Mexican Dam" (a deteriorating, low concrete dam), a possible place to pause and explore.

Continue south on the main road. Look ahead to spot the road and powerlines swinging left uphill (east) and turn right, off the main road, about 100 feet before the powerlines and the road turn away from the river. Your right turn will be at just under 1 3/4 miles from your starting point, only a few hundred feet past Mexican Dam. Soon after you make the turn you will be riding south along the river's edge. The ride ends at a gate blocking the road, at just over 2 1/2 miles. From here, for an easy ride just turn around and retrace your route back; for a longer ride look for side trips around the river and for a harder ride consider some exploring up into the hills away from the river.

Ride #38
CLEAR
CREEK ROAD

Difficulty: Intermediate
Distance: 9 1/2 miles
Starting Elevation: 4750 feet
Highest Elevation: 5550 feet
Map: USGS Genoa 7.5

Trailhead
Drive south, through Carson City, to the intersection of U.S. 395 and U.S. 50 (50 goes to Lake Tahoe via Spooner Summit). Continue south on 395 for a few hundred feet past the intersection and turn right onto Clear Creek Road. Park along Clear Creek Road, near its intersection with U.S. 395.

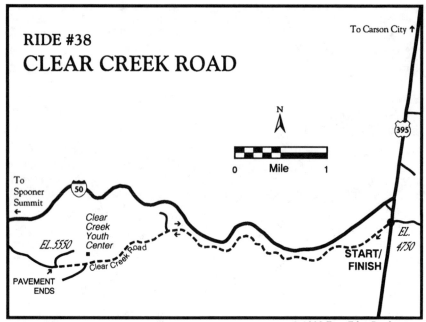

RIDE #38
CLEAR CREEK ROAD

To Carson City ↑

N

0   Mile   1

To
Spooner
Summit
←

50

Clear
Creek
Youth
Center

EL.5550

Clear Creek Road

PAVEMENT
ENDS

START/
FINISH

EL.
4750

395

© 1993 Fine Edge Productions

Difficulty

A trip to where the pavement ends is usually what most cyclists will do on this road— it provides a gently climbing, very scenic aerobic ride on "non-maintained", low-traffic pavement (it actually appears to be at least moderately maintained). It is possible to use it for a road bike workout, but bumps and cracks will require much closer attention for road bikes than for mountain bikes if you are to avoid wheel damage. This is an out and back ride (total mileage of 9 1/2 miles), with an elevation gain of 800 feet on the 4 3/4 miles out. Clear Creek Road is suited to intermediate riders or better.

Description

This ride courses up a beautiful canyon, one with some remarkable rock formations in the first half. It follows what remains of the old highway up to

Clear Creek rock formation.

Spooner Summit. From the intersection of U.S. 395 and Clear Creek Road, head west on Clear Creek. At two miles you will cross a cattleguard— continue ahead. At three miles you will pass a road going off to the right (to houses). Continue up the main road, along the creek. At just over 4 1/4 miles you will cross another cattleguard.

At 4 1/2 miles, you'll pass a smaller dirt road headed left— continue ahead on the main road. This ride ends at 4 3/4 miles (dirt road ahead, pavement swings to the right and into the Clear Creek Youth Center). Simply turn around and enjoy the long downhill to your starting point for a total mileage of 9 1/2 miles.

For the adventurous and for a longer/ harder ride, you can continue ahead from the turnaround point onto the dirt road— it is possible to keep going west. You will encounter bits and pieces of pavement, caved in and washed out areas, some places where you have to carry your bike, and some steep climbing (absolutely not for road bikes!). Depending upon what you like in mountain biking, exploring on up the road here can be anything from entertaining to painfully arduous. If you make it all the way, the remains of this old road will come out on U.S. 50 at an elevation of 6965, about one mile east of Spooner Summit (and U.S. 50 offers you an alternate route back to the beginning of this ride).

View from Kings Canyon.

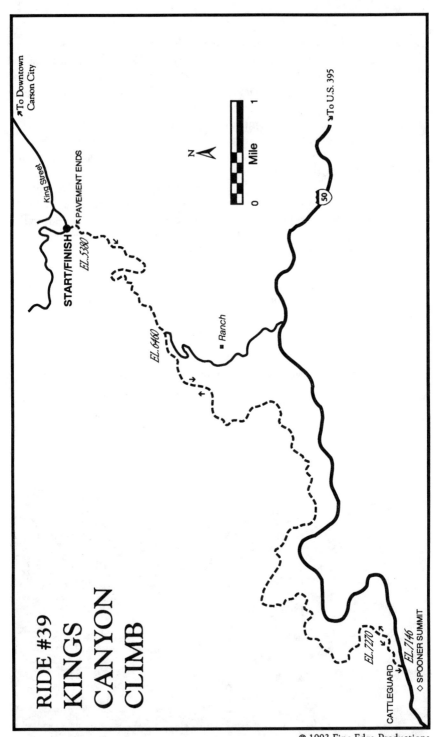

RIDE #39
KINGS
CANYON
CLIMB

To Downtown
Carson City

King Street

START/FINISH
PAVEMENT ENDS
EL. 5580

EL. 6460

Ranch

50

To U.S. 395

N

0   Mile   1

CATTLEGUARD
EL. 7270
EL. 7146
◇ SPOONER SUMMIT

© 1993 Fine Edge Productions

Ride #39 KINGS CANYON CLIMB

Difficulty: Advanced
Distance: 19 miles
Starting Elevation: 5380 feet
Highest Elevation: 7270 feet
Map: USGS Carson City/Genoa 7.5

Trailhead

To get to the trailhead for this ride, you first need to get on King Street in Carson City. It runs west, directly from the Nevada State Capitol (domed building). However, it no longer comes through to U.S. 395 (Carson Street)—

it starts one block west. To get onto King Street turn west one block before or one block after the Capitol Building (Musser Street or Second Street), go a few blocks, then turn one block to King Street. Follow King west until the pavement ends (three miles from downtown). Park just off the blacktop.

Difficulty

This ride is suited to advanced riders or better. Technically it is not particularly difficult, but it is long (9 1/2 miles each way, for a total ride of 19 miles) and the ride up to the road's end at Spooner Summit (U.S. 50) involves an altitude gain of about 1900 feet. Many cyclists do not ride King's Canyon as an out and back— they have someone drop them off on top and they ride 9 1/2 miles back to the pavement,

Ride through the forest.

virtually all flat or downhill after the first one-half mile.

Description

This is a delightful ride. It begins in the foothills and ends in a mountain forest. The entire route is on a non-maintained jeep road, so there is not a lot of traffic to contend with. At the trailhead, the end of the pavement, there are roads going right and left. The road to the right is gated and climbs very steeply up through private land to a mine. Take the road going left (south). Stay on this main road, climbing steadily and sometimes steeply. You will achieve two-thirds of your elevation gain in the first three miles (over 400 feet per mile).

At just under 2 1/2 miles you will encounter a fork— the left goes downhill to a giant meadow and a ranch, the right is your route (continues climbing). Shortly after the fork, there is a breathtaking view to the south! At just under three miles you will enter National Forest. After four miles, the climbing eases and there is about three miles of fairly flat riding, followed by some more steep sections. At just under nine miles, you will reach your maximum elevation (7270) and start a brief downhill to the highway. When you cross the cattleguard just prior to the pavement you will have ridden 9 1/2 miles.

For an out and back, turn around and retrace the route that brought you to Spooner Summit. If you would like a different road back to your starting point and don't mind pavement and the possibility of lots of traffic, you can descend back to U.S. 395 on U.S. 50 (nine miles). When you reach 395, ride north to pick up King Street (three miles), then west to where you began (another three miles). This loop increases the total ride from 19 to 24 1/2 miles.

City view from the Carson Range.

APPENDIX A
IMBA RULES OF THE TRIAL

1. RIDE ON OPEN TRAILS ONLY
Respect trail and road closures (ask if not sure), avoid possible trespass on private land. Obtain permits and authorization as may be required, Federal and State wilderness areas are closed to cycling. Additional trails may be closed because of sensitive environmental concerns or conflicts with other users. Your riding example will determine what is closed to all cyclists!

2. LEAVE NO TRACE
Be sensitive to the dirt beneath you. Even on open trails, you should not ride under conditions where you will leave evidence of your passing, such as on certain soils shortly after a rain. Observe the different types of soils and trail construction; practice low-impact cycling. This also means staying on the trail and not creating any new ones. Be sure to pack out at least as much as you pack in.

3. CONTROL YOUR BICYCLE!
Inattention for even a second can cause disaster. Excessive speed maims and threatens people; there is no excuse for it!

4. ALWAYS YIELD TRAIL
Make known your approach well in advance. A friendly greeting (or bell) is considerate and works well; startling someone may cause loss of trail access. Show your respect when passing others by slowing to a walk or even stopping. Anticipate that other trail users may be around corners or in blind spots.

5. NEVER SPOOK ANIMALS
All animals are startled by an unannounced approach, a sudden movement, or a loud noise. This can be dangerous for you, others, and the animals. Give animals extra room and time to adjust to you. In passing, use special care and follow the directions of horseback riders (ask if uncertain). Running cattle and disturbing wild animals is a serious offense. Leave gates as you found them, or as marked.

6. PLAN AHEAD
Know your equipment, your ability, and the area in which you are riding— and prepare accordingly. Be self-sufficient at all times, keep your machine in good repair, and carry necessary supplies for changes in weather or other conditions. A well-executed trip is a satisfaction to you and not a burden or offense to others. Keep trails open by setting an example of responsible cycling for all mountain bicyclists.

APPENDIX B

THE CARE AND FEEDING OF A MOUNTAIN BIKE

ROUTINE CHECKUPS FOR YOUR BICYCLE.

The key to years of fun and fitness from your mountain bike is giving it checkups on a regular basis. You need to know how to clean it, lubricate a few places, make simple adjustments, and recognize when something needs expert attention. For the average rider, most bike shops recommend tune-ups once a year and complete overhauls every two to three years. All of the maintenance in between your trips to the bike shop you can do yourself. Given below is a nine-step checkup procedure, a list to run through after every extensive ride, before you head back out into the hills again.

1. CLEAN-UP

Unless the frame is really filthy, use a soft rag and a non-corrosive wax/polish such as Pledge to wipe off the grime and bring the old shine back. If you need to use water or soap and water prior to the polish, don't high pressure spray directly at any of the bearing areas (pedals, hubs, bottom bracket or head set). You should clean all your components too (including the chain and the rear cogs), but use a different rag and a lubricant such as Tri-Flow or Finish Line for wiping them down. Do not use polish or lubricants to clean your rims— an oily film will reduce your braking ability. Instead, wipe off the rims with a clean dry rag. If you need to remove rubber deposits from the sidewalls of the rims use acetone as a solvent.

2. INSPECTION

After you get the grit and grime off, check out the frame very carefully, looking for bulges or cracks. If there are chips or scratches that expose bare metal (especially when the metal is steel) use automotive or bicycle touch up paint to cover them up. Your inspection should also include the components. Look for broken, bent or otherwise visibly damaged parts. Pay special attention to the wheels. When you spin them, watch the rim where it passes the brake pads. Look for wobbles and hops, and if there is a lot of movement, the wheel needs to be trued at home (or take it to a bike shop) before using it. Look for loose or broken spokes. And finally, carefully check your tires for sidewall damage, for heavy tread wear, and for cuts and bulges, glass and nails, thorns or whatever.

3. BRAKES

Grab the brakes and make sure they don't feel mushy and that the pads are contacting the rim firmly (be certain the brake pads do not rub against the tires!). If the brakes don't feel firm, there are barrel adjusters at one or both ends of the wire cables that control the brakes— turn them counterclockwise to take up some of the slack. If you are unsure as to the dependability of your brakes, for safety's sake let a bike shop check them.

Rancho San Rafael Park Canyon singletrack.

4. BEARING AREAS

Most cyclists depend upon professional mechanics to fix any problems in the pedals, hubs, bottom bracket or head set, but they should be able to recognize when something is wrong. Spin the wheels, spin the crankarms (and the pedals) and move the handlebars from side to side. If you feel notches or grittiness, or if you hear snapping, grating or clicking noises, you have a problem. Check to make sure each of the four areas is properly tightened. To check for looseness try to wiggle a crankarm side to side or try to move a wheel side to side. Check your headset adjustment by holding the front brake, rocking the bike forward and backward and listening for clunking sounds.

5. SHIFTING

Presuming your bike has gears, check to make sure you can use all of them. The most common problem is the stretching of the inner wire which operates the rear derailleur. If your bike is not shifting properly try turning the barrel adjuster which is located where the cable comes out of the derailleur. Turn it just a little, and usually a counterclockwise direction is what you need. Unless you know what you are doing, avoid turning the little adjustment screws on the derailleurs.

6. NUTS AND BOLTS

Make sure the nuts and bolts which hold everything together are tight. The handlebars and stem should not move around under pressure, and neither should your saddle. And make certain that the axle nuts or quick releases that hold your wheels are fully secure— when a wheel falls off, the result is almost always crashtime. If you have quick release hubs, they operate as follows: Mostly tighten them by holding the nut and winding the lever, but finish the job by swinging the lever over like a clamp (it's spring loaded). Do not wind them up super tight like you would with a wingnut—for safe operation they must be clamped, and clamped very securely, with considerable spring tension! If you are at all uncertain regarding the use of quick releases, go by a bike shop and ask for a demonstration.

7. ACCESSORIES

Make sure all your accessories, from water bottles to bags to pumps to lights, are operational and secure. Systematically check them all out and if you carry flat fixing or other on-the-road repair materials or tools, make sure you've got what you need and you know how to use what you carry. Statistics show that over 90% of all bicycle breakdowns are the result of flat tires, so it is recommended that you carry a pump, a spare tube, a patch kit, and a couple of tire levers with you whenever you ride.

8. LUBRICATION

The key to long-term mechanical happiness for you and your bike is proper and frequent lubrication. The most important area of lubrication is the chain— spray it with a Teflon-based or other synthetic oil (WD-40, household oil, and motor oil are not recommended), then wipe off all the excess. You can use the same lubricant for very sparsely coating the moving parts of your brakes and derailleurs.

9. INFLATION

You now are ready for the last step. Improper inflation can lead to blowouts or pinch flats. Read the side of your tires to see what the recommended pressure is and fill them up. If there is a range of pressures given, use the high figure for street cycling, the low figure or near it for off-road riding. After going through these nine steps of getting your bike ready you've earned another good long ride!

Everybody knows how to ride a bike— at least most everybody can ride around the neighborhood. But with the advent of the mountain bike, riding a two-wheel pedal powered machine has gotten more complicated. Watch a pro-level mountain bike race and the need for "technical skills" will become obvious. Can you handle steep hills, big rocks, creeks, muddy bogs, loose sand, big tree roots, deep gravel, or radical washboards? These are the kinds of factors that differentiate mountain biking from road riding and that demand skills and balance above and beyond those required to ride around the neighborhood. The key to acquiring these abilities is practice— start easy and work diligently until you achieve high-level control of your bike.

Long Valley Loop Oasis.

APPENDIX C
BASIC SKILLS FOR MOUNTAIN BIKING

1. BICYCLE
All mountain bikes are not created equal. Some are better suited to staying on pavement. They have too much weight, too long a wheelbase, ineffective braking systems, sloppy shifting, too smooth of tread on the tires, poorly welded frames, and so on. As a general rule, the mountain bicycles marketed by the discount store chains, department stores, and sporting goods stores are only suited to on-road, non-abusive use. Bicycles from bike stores, excepting their least expensive models, are generally suited to heavy duty, skilled off-road use. They should be relatively light (under 30 pounds), and have a fairly short wheelbase and chainstay (for agility), moderately steep head angle (again for agility), strong and dependable braking and shifting systems, well-made frames, and knobby/aggressive tires. For details on choosing the right bike for you, consult the experts at your local bike shop. They can help you not only with selecting a bicycle, but also with various accessory decisions, in such areas as suspension forks, bar ends, and gear ratio changes. And of extreme importance, whatever bike you decide on, get the right size for you. If a bike is too big for your height and weight, no matter how hard you try yourself will never be able to properly handle it. If you are in doubt or in between sizes, for serious off-road riding opt for the smaller bike.

2. FUNDAMENTAL PRINCIPLES
There are some very general rules for off-road riding that apply all the time. The first, "ride in control", is fundamental to everything else. Balance is the key to keeping a bike upright— when you get out of control you will lose your ability to balance the bike (that is crash). Control is directly related to speed and excessive speed for the conditions you are facing is the precursor to loss of control. When in doubt, slow down!

The second principle for off-road riding is "read the trail ahead". In order to have time to react to changes in the trail surface and to obstacles, you should be looking ahead 10 to 15 feet. Especially as your speed increases, you want to avoid being surprised by hazardous trail features (rocks, logs, roots, ruts, and so on)—if you see them well ahead, you can pick a line to miss them, slow down to negotiate them, or even stop to walk over or around them.

The third principle is to "stay easy on the grips". One of the most common reactions by novices in tough terrain is to severely tense up, most noticeably in a "death grip" on the handlebars. This level of tightness not only leads to hand, arm and shoulder discomfort but interferes with fluid, supple handling of the bike. Grip loosely and bend at the elbows a bit—don't fight the bicycle, work with it!

The last general principle to be presented here is "plan your shifting". If you are

Old wooden flume in Rancho San Rafael Park.

looking ahead on the trail, there should be no shifting "surprises". Anticipate hills, especially steep ascents, and shift before your drivetrain comes under a strong load. Mountain bikes have a lot of gears and their proper use will make any excursion more enjoyable.

3. CLIMBING

Mountain bikes were originally single-speed, balloon-tired cruisers taken by truck or car to the top of a hill and then used for exciting and rapid descent. After a few years, to eliminate the shuttle they were given gears. Today's off-road bikes have 18 to 24 speeds, with a few extremely low gears so they can climb very steep hills. One of the keys to long or difficult climbs is "attitude"—it's a mental thing, in that you need to be able to accept an extended, aerobic challenge with the thoughts "I can do it" and "this is fun".

Your bike is made with hill climbing in mind. Find a gear and a pace that is tolerable (not anaerobic) and try to maintain it. Pick a line ahead, stay relaxed, and anticipate shifting, as noted earlier. In addition, be alert to problems in weight distribution that occur when climbing. It is best to stay seated, keeping your weight solidly over the traction (rear) wheel if possible. However, if the slope is so steep that the front wheel lifts off of the ground you will have to lean forward and slide toward the front of the saddle. Constant attention to weight distribution will give you optimum traction and balance for a climb. And make sure your saddle height is positioned so when your foot is at the bottom of a pedal stroke, your knee is very slightly bent— a saddle too low or too high will significantly reduce both power and control on a steep and difficult climb.

4. DESCENDING

This is where most serious accidents occur, primarily because a downhill lends itself to high speed. It is unquestionably the most exciting part of mountain bike riding— expert riders reach speeds up to 60 mph! For descents, the "stay in control" and "read the trail ahead" principles can be injury-saving. Know your ability and don't exceed it. And be certain your brakes are in good working order—don't believe the slogan "brakes are for sissies"— on steep and difficult downhills everyone has to use them. Regarding braking, always apply the rear brake before the front (to avoid an "endo", that is, flying over the handlebars), and if possible, brake in spurts rather than "dragging" them. On easy hills, practice using your brakes to get comfortable with them.

As was the case for steep uphills, steep descents require attention to weight distribution. Many riders lower their saddle an inch or two prior to descending (to get a lower center of gravity). All cyclists quickly learn to lift their weight slightly off the saddle and shift it back a few inches to keep traction and to avoid the feeling of being on the verge of catapulting over the handlebars— practice this weight transfer on smooth but steep downhills so you can do it comfortably later on obstacle-laden terrain. Finally, it is possible to go too slow on a difficult downhill, so slow you can't "blast" over obstacles. Instead, because of lack of momentum, hazards can bring you to an abrupt stop or twist your front wheel, and both of these results can cause loss of control.

5. TURNING

A particularly treacherous time for mountain bikers is high speed or obstacle-

Sometimes it's just too steep!

Steamboat Ditch Trail.

laden turns. The first principle is don't enter a curve too fast. Turns often contain loose dirt and debris created by all the mountain bikes that preceded you. Slow down before you get to it; you can always accelerate during the turn if you choose. Lean around the turn as smoothly as possible, always keeping an eye out for obstacles. It is common for the rear wheel to skid in turns. To take the fright out of that phenomenon, go find a gentle turn with soft dirt and practice skidding to learn how you and your bike will respond.

6. OBSTACLES

If you get into the real spirit of off-road cycling, you will not ride just on smooth, groomed trails. You will encounter rocks, roots, limbs, logs, trenches, ruts, washboards, loose sand (or dirt or gravel), and water in a variety of forms from snow and ice to mud bogs to free-flowing springs and creeks. Obviously, the easiest means for handling an obstacle is to go around it; however, you can't always do that. For raised obstacles, those you need to get up and over, riders need to learn to "pop the front wheel". To practice this, find a low curb or set out a 4x4 piece of lumber. Approach it, and just before the front wheel impacts it, rapidly push down then pull up the front wheel. The wheel lift is enhanced if you simultaneously lower and raise your torso and apply a hard pedal stroke. After your front wheel clears the obstacle, shift your weight up and forward a little so the rear wheel can bounce over it lightly.

If you encounter "washboards", the key to relatively painless negotiating is to maintain a moderate speed and get into a shock absorbing posture— slightly up and off the saddle, knees slightly bent, elbows slightly bent, loose grip on the handlebars, and relaxed. Soft spots in the trail can make your bike difficult to control and create an instant slowdown. If you have to deal with loose, deep sand, dirt or gravel, the key is to go slower but "power through". Shift your weight back a little (for better traction), then keep your bike straight and keep pedaling. Maintaining momentum and a straight line is also important in mud holes, and be certain to do any shifting prior to soft spots or muddy bogs (otherwise you will lose momentum). Sharp turns can present a particular problem in these conditions— you will be much more prone to losing the rear wheel to a slide out, so be extra cautious in sandy or muddy curves.

Going through water can be a lot of fun, or it can be a rude awakening if you end up upsidedown on a cold February afternoon. Before any attempt to cross a waterway, stop and examine it first. Make sure it isn't so deep that it will abruptly stop you, then find the route that has the least obstacles (look for deep holes, big rocks, and deep sand). Approach the crossing at a fairly low speed and plan on pedaling through it (rather than coasting) for maximum traction and control. Be aware of the potential for harmful effects that riding through water can have on your bearings (if they are not sealed) and exposed moving parts— plan on lubricating your chain, derailleurs, inner wires, and so on, when you return home. Finally, regarding snow and ice, as much as possible just stay away from ice. Snow riding can be fun but if it's deep, it can be very laborious. Maintaining momentum and avoiding buried obstacles are the two major tasks for snow riders. Also, the difficulty of steep ascents and descents are significantly magnified by a few inches of snow— most mountain bikers riding on snow prefer flat or nearly flat terrain.

Rancho San Rafael Canyon.

TOPO MAPS & GUIDE BOOKS FROM FINE EDGE PRODUCTIONS

MOUNTAIN BIKING & RECREATION TOPO MAPS
Six Color, Double-Sided, Includes Trail Profiles & Route Descriptions
NEW! Eastern High Sierra-Mammoth, June, Mono $9.95
NEW! Santa Monica Mountains $8.95
NEW! Santa Ana Mountains, Cleveland N.F. (10/93) $8.95
    San Gabriel Mountains– West $8.95
    North Lake Tahoe Basin $8.95
    South Lake Tahoe Basin..$8.95

GUIDE BOOKS
Mountain Biking the High Sierra
    Guide 1, Owens Valley and Inyo County, 2nd Ed. by Douglass $8.95
    Guide 2, Mammoth Lakes and Mono County, 3rd Ed. by Douglass...................$8.95
    Guide 3A, Lake Tahoe South, 3rd Ed. by Bonser & Miskimins $8.95
    Guide 3B, Lake Tahoe North, 2nd Ed. by Bonser $8.95
NEW! Guide 13, Reno/Carson Valley by Miskimins $10.95

Mountain Biking the Coast Range
NEW! Guide 4, Ventura County and the Sespe, 3rd Ed.,by McTigue $8.95
    Guide 5, Santa Barbara County, 3rd Ed. by McTigue & Douglass $8.95
NEW! Guide 7, Santa Monica Mountains, 2nd Ed. by Hasenauer & Langton $8.95
    Guide 8, Saugus Dist., Angeles N.F. with Mt. Pinos by Troy & Woten $8.95
    Guide 9, San Gabriel Mountains, Angeles N.F. by Troy $8.95
NEW! Guide 10, San Bernardino Mountains by Shipley $8.95
NEW! Guide 11, Orange County and Cleveland N.F. by Rassmussen $8.95
NEW! Guide 12, Riverside Co. & Coachella Valley by Maag & Shipley (10/93) $8.95

OTHER BOOKS & MAPS AVAILABLE
NEW! Mountain Biking Southern California's Best 100 Trails $14.95
    Favorite Pedal Tours of Northern California, by Bloom $12.95
    Marin-Sonoma Counties Map, California $7.95
    Excelsior Dist. Tahoe N.F., Hwy 80 Map...$6.95
    Crystal Basin, Eldorado N.F., Hwy 50 Map..$6.95
    Moab, Utah, Slick Rock $5.95
    Ski Touring the Eastern High Sierra by Douglass & Lombardo $8.95
    Exploring California's Channel Islands, an Artist's View by Gates $6.95
NEW! CAPE HORN, One Man's Dream, One Woman's Nightmare
    by Hemingway-Douglass (9/93) $24.95

To order any of these items, see your local dealer or order direct from
Fine Edge Productions. Please include $2.00 for shipping with check or money order.
California residents add 7.25% state sales tax. 20% discount on orders of 5 or more items.
Fine Edge Productions, Route 2, Box 303, Bishop, California 93514.
(619)387-2412 / FAX (619)387-2286.

FINE EDGE
Productions
BISHOP, CALIFORNIA